LANGUAGE *Matters*

Books by Tony Quagliano

Language Drawn and Quartered, Ghost Dance Press, 1975
Fierce Meadows, Petronium Press, 1981
Snail Mail Poems, Tinfish Network, 1998
pictographs, red moon press, 2008

LANGUAGE *Matters*

Tony Quagliano

SELECTED POETRY

The New York Quarterly Foundation, Inc.
New York, New York

tonyquaglianopoetryfund.com

NYQ Books™ is an imprint of The New York Quarterly Foundation, Inc.

The New York Quarterly Foundation, Inc.
P. O. Box 2015
Old Chelsea Station
New York, NY 10113

www.nyqbooks.org

First Edition

Set in ITC New Baskerville Std

Cover art and book design: Laura Ruby. Rainwear (drawing, 1990) interweaves the sheer pali (cliffs) where ancient Hawaiian warriors jumped to their violent deaths and the boot-clad nurturers of that now-pastoral landscape.

Library of Congress Control Number: 2009937435

ISBN: 978-1-935520-08-5

The Image and the Word

Picture this if you will: the words we know, all the words we have acquired along with the ways of connecting them in all our respective cultures, are nothing less than the irreducible expression of a singular nature we call human.

We are selves in a world because we have words.

Tony Quagliano
1941–2007

Acknowledgements

Grateful acknowledgment is given to the following magazines and anthologies where these poems originally appeared:

Magazines: *Ab Intra, Aethlon: The Journal of Sport Literature, Ant, Artbeat–Guide to Hawaii Artists, Artful Dodge, Arts: A Publication of the Garden Island Arts Council, Assembling, Azami, Bamboo Ridge (Malama–Hawaiian Land and Water), Be-Bop and Beyond, Big Boulevard, Bitterroot, Black Mountain II Review, Brooklyn Review, California Quarterly, Chaminade Literary Review, Cicada, City and County of Honolulu Poetry on TheBus, Cutting Edge Quarterly, Elysian Fields Quarterly, Event, Exquisite Corpse, Floating Island, Frogpond, Ghost Dance, Hapa, Harvard Review, Hawai'i Review, Hawaii Jazz Preservation Society Newsletter, Hawaii Literary Arts Council Newsletter, Holy Doors–An Anthology of Poetry, Prose and Criticism, Honolulu Journal, Honolulu Star-Bulletin and Advertiser, Hui O Laka–Newsletter of the Koke'e Natural History Museum, Humanities News, Hummingbird, Impact, Invisible City, Japanophile, Jama– The Journal of the American Medical Association, Journalism Quarterly, Kaimana–The Journal of the Hawaii Literary Arts Council, Kayak, Kerouac Connection, Language and Culture, Laugh Literary and Man the Humping Guns, Lie$ Not Journal, Literary Arts Hawaii, Long Island Quarterly, Meatball, Mele, Midatlantic Review, Minotaur, Modern Haiku, Moody Street Irregulars, Negative Capability (The Big Easy Crescent City That Care Forgot), New Directions, New York Quarterly, Oahu Review, The Pan American Review, Prime Time–Hawaii Newspaper Agency, Phantasm, Pyramid, Ramrod, Rattle, The Redneck Review, River King–Poetry Supplement, Rolling Stock, Rolling Stone, Romanticism and Modernity–A Humanities Guide, The San Francisco Quarterly, Schist, Small Press Review, Snakeroots, Solo, Southern Poetry Review, The Sprit that Moves Us (Free Parking), Spitball, Spring–The Journal of the E.E. Cummings Society, Star-Web Paper, Texas Observer, Tinfish, Vagabond, Volcano Gazette, Wallace Stevens Journal, Western Review, Wormwood Review,* and *Yankee.*

Anthologies: *American Sings,* 1962; *Fire in the Sea,* editor Sue Cowing, 1996; *Essays in Creativity and Science,* editor Diana DeLuca, 1986; *Haiku Compass: Directions in the Poetical Map of U.S.A.,* editor William Higginson, 1994; *Heiwa,* editors Jiro Nakano and Brien Hallett, 1995; *Honolulu Stories,* editor Gavan Daws, 2008; *Only Connect,* editors Guy Amirthanayagam and S.C. Harrex, 1981; *Perceiving Nature,* editor Diana DeLuca, 1988; *Poet Dreaming in the Artist's House,* editors Emily Buchwald and Ruth Roston, 1984; *Poetry Hawaii: A Contemporary Anthology,* editors Frank Stewart and John Unterecker, 1979; *Poetry Now Poets Palette,* editor Kerrie Pateman, 1994; *Poetry of Solitude–A Tribute to Edward Hopper,* editor Gail Levin, 1995; *Pushcart Prize–Best of the Small Presses I,* editor Bill Henderson, 1976; *Visiting Dr. Williams: Poems Inspired by the Life and Work of William Carlos Williams,* editors Thom Tammaro and Sheila Coghill, 2009; *Visiting Wallace–Poems Inspired by the Life and Work of Wallace Stevens,* editors Dennis Barone and James Finnegan, 2009, and *New Hungers for Old: One-Hundred Years of Italian-American Poetry,* editor Dennis Barone, 2011.

Contents

I. Hawaii
Cliffs   13

Bio-Politics of Molokai   15
The Ancient Murmurs in the Blood Meadows   16
One for William Carlos Williams in Hawaii   17
Fierce Meadows   18
In Honolulu My Minimum   19
The Leper Eye   20
The Sand Sculptor   21
Concert   22
Waiting at Gate–Honolulu Airport   23
Six Poems After the Honolulu Peace Conference   24
Alzheimer's   26
A Haole Writes One Local Poem   27
The Condo Marxist   28
The Ride to Ho'omaluhia   29
On the Ambulance Run   30
|| Jazz Note || 31
When You're at Koke'e   32
The Light on Monhegan, on Kauai   33
On Diamond Head, the Morning Rain   34
On Mauna Kea   35
Meanwhile I Just Said to Myself   36

II. Synaptic Trails
The Night Tide   39

A Biological Theory of History   41
What Primeval Terror Has the Gentle Man Known   42
Bashing Neanderthals   43
Nerve Stone Discourse   44
Biopoetics   45
Construction in Congratulations to the Electronic Bi-ped
   Striding Toward the Frontiers of Language   46
Experimental Language   48
Adding "Poetry" to Chaos Theory
   To Find a Poem   49
Oldenburg, Heisenberg and Oscar "Shotgun" Albarado   50

Man Alone the Beast 52
Hawk and Rock 54
On Idealization of Nature 55
What to Do with Scenery 56

III. **Only If Something Matters**
In My Brother's Coat 59

Some Guy Named Ludwig 61
Turning Over in His Grave 62
The Phoenix Myth 63
Celestial Mechanics 64
I Read This Poem about Geometry 65
Dr. Patterson Speaks with Koko Before an Audience of
    International Scientists 66
Sad Tropes 68
Say Jazz 71
Not the Uppers or the Downers 72
Papa's Existential Etiquette 73
To the Author of "To My Brother Miguel" 74
The Edward Hopper Retrospective 76
Early Onset 78
Heraclitus Once 79
Between a Rock and Mahatma Gandhi 80

IV. **Poetry of Politics : Politics of Poetry**
Witness for Peace 83

The Will Behind the Knife 85
Semiotic Self-Deconstruction 86
To the Manifesto Crowd 87
The Socialist 88
Four Political Questions 90
The Redistribution 91
The Suffix as Meaning 92
Hall of Fame 95
Right Attack 96
The Teeth of the Mask 99
One 100
This Man's Castle 101
Winslow Homer, War Illustrator 102

Sinéad O'Connor   103
"Twenty Cents and Curtains"   104
Ivy Manoa   105
Get Out of Poetry by Sundown   106
The Survivalist   108
On the Way to the Writing Workshop   109
On Bly on Poetry   110
The New Formal Poetry   111
Recollections of a Coot   112
Poets in the Schools   113
Renshi (Linked Free Verse)
    In the '90's   114
Snail Mail Poems   116
Short-Short on the New Anthology   117
The New Lit Mag   118
No Ideas but in Things   119
The Underground Press   120
Poetry Money   121
The Travelling Regionalist   122
Victory at Sea   124
You Can Tell "Creative Writers"   125
The Showdown   126

V. **Word-Dance for Poets and Poseurs**
A Jazz Note   131

    For Doctor WCW   133
    Hardly a Poem   134
    An Occasional Poem to Czeslaw Milosz   135
    13 Ways of Avoiding
        A Derivative Poetry Cliché   136
    On Asked for Writing Advice   137
    Ezra Pound in Hawaii   138
    On Detractors of Kerouac   139
    Letter from Hawaii to David Ray   140
    On Bukowski Elegies
        And the Dipshit Clowns
        Who Write Them   142
    On Andrei Codrescu's "Writers"   143
    The Night I Let Bukowski Live   144
    Another of the Wisdom Boys   145

Bunny Mullins Poet Laureate
    Not in My Name   146
A Fable for "Creative Writers"   147
On New Academics Foisting a New Moronicity   148
Hard Guy in the Faculty Lounge   149
Who's the Real Slim Talent   150
Some Boondockers   152
Language Poet at the Baseball Game   153
On Poetry   154
Andrei's Shtick on Letterman   155
Raymond Chandler   156
Investigative Reporter   159
The Genius Award for a Life's Work
    Of Elaborated Signage   160
Feed the Hungry, or
    Do Something Better   161
Last Chance Poem for Wing Tek Lum   162
Kesey on Kerouac on TV   164
To Kerouac   166
Benjamin Latrobe in New Orleans   167
Ezra's ABC's, and Deeds   168
Illimitable Country   170
One for WCW at the Post-
    Nuclear Philosophy
    Conference in Manoa   171

VI. Poetry Overheard
One Still Treescape   173

Wolfsbane for Cantwell   175
Intro to Camarillo Kate   178
Real Class   179
Post Op   180
Getting By   182
Her Blues   184
At the Artiste Bar   185
Shack Job   186
How I know   187
The Typo in the Tattoo Parlor
    L-O-V-E and H-A-T-S   188
The Great Turtle Priest on Television   190

Medical News on the Night 192
For Carl Furillo 193
Making Light 194
At the Fairgrounds Bar 196
The Botanists 197
The Wacko and the Shrink 198
Deconstructing a Disgusting
    Dirty Filthy Poem 200
The Vapors 201
Noir Letter to The Swede 202
Musial and the Bums 204
Sure, That's It 205

VII. Illimitable Country: Other Places, Other Poems
Ah, to Be East 209

Brighton-Manhattan Transit 211
Carnival Parlay 212
A Cold Walk Home 213
Krait Coiled in the Bedsheet 214
That November 215
A Brooklyn Dodger Fan in 1988 216
Color Line 217
A Cold Rain Obscures L.A. Tonight 218
No Handle on the Night 219
Ancient Gringo Savvy 220
Bus Ride Notes 222
Driving Through Donner Pass 223
Take a Magic Word Like Tundra 224
Society Island 225
Gauguin 226
Papeete Poem 227
A Jazz Note (N'awlins) 228
No Bullets in the Sky Tonight 229
Night Sky Piano 230
Edward Hopper's Lighthouse at Two Lights, 1927 231
Quick Cities of Shadows 232
To See Shoah 233

About the Author 236

I. *Hawaii*

The sheer
dead fall
cliffs of
Hawai'i
plummet through
the wild red air

nobody catches
all their
names

Bio-Politics of Molokai

if the chinese brought leprosy to paradise
why say so? did they want it
to give or have
any more than you or me?

if the british brought syphilis to paradise
why say so? did they want it
to give or have
any more than you or me?

if a thousand years of european serfdom
brought indentured slavery to paradise
why say so? could they have valued labor
any more than you or me?

if the shriven congregationals of honolulu
shunned the belgian papist for his pride
losing themselves forever, are they lost
any more than you or me?

besides, the leprosy might have been east asian
the syphilis french, slavery american
class arrogance polynesian, and if eternal
damnation is equally distributed among all
the peoples of all the world, isn't that

aloha spirit, the rainbow truth
of paradise, of leprous molokai the friendly isle
and would anyone want it otherwise
any more than you or me?

The Ancient Murmurs in the Blood Meadows

On Diamond Head
the morning rain has started
swept leeward by the daily trades
which certainly will later sweep
across the lava rock
the ghost trails   the ancient
murmurs in the blood meadows
the spirit in the new steel
jet paths   coral reefs
the tourist wash
the mainland asia polynesia
certainly will later sweep
some blue and white
amazing sky

One for William Carlos Williams in Hawaii

the way the wagon runs
down the rain
here
if you use the word
color
it ruins the word blue

Fierce Meadows

On Oahu I should try something
rural and lyrical filled
with bright birds skittering
through a bamboo grove after
dawn rain in the mountains
or decry
the scattering of ghosts
and warrior bones
the steely rout of magic places
peace and healing
but it's no use here
behind my pale and desecrating eyes.
Blood deep in the lava rock
fierce meadows of warrior bones.

In Honolulu my minimum

In Honolulu my minimum
daily requirement is
oxygen, nutriment
shade and time
to develop reasons

the spoor of grace

the slate
quarrying in Tipperary
is fine
but it's such a long way to go

The Leper Eye

"And then it happened, the mark
of the beast was laid upon him."
                    Jack London, "The Sheriff of Kona"

The federal doctors in the old territory
developed the leper eye
mad Calvinists seeking signs
of evil in the universe
flesh elected somewhere to be lost
horror and slow decay
of the living temple, vessel
of grace, image of god

seven year incubation
then, the darkening
above the eyes
the peculiar shine on the darkening
the featureless face
hands without fingers
arms without hands
the blossoming horror

the walking horror with bells on
once a test of Christ
the lion face
roaring horror prowling paradise
by the nightmare light
of the leper eye

The Sand Sculptor

Blake knew the indissoluble connectedness
of everything
innocence to experience
heaven to hell
and us here, somewhere
connected to both
he knew the sacred linkage
of each thing to all things
"the universe in a grain of sand"

as the sand sculptor orders and forms
his billion grains of sand
into a structure of universes

he links a child in Rhode Island
to Hawaii now
he links Atlantic and Pacific
the earth to the sea
even links the brute vandal
to the artful maker
the urge to create order
under the random wheeling sky

he links the passersby
to himself and to each other
links each of us
to all of us
and each of us
to ourselves

Concert

The bottom of the harpsichord
is magnesium
have you seen
what makes this instrument
unlike all others? it's
the frame
magnesium, kneel
to see it
nuzzle the surprising
metal, while on top
a broad and cloudy wall on wood
Mexico on flute
Vienna Minnesota
Paris Honolulu.

In green Manoa thick
with transplants
pungent foliage warmed
by wide rain and tradewinds under
a sky of Ko'olaus and clouds
formed in the currents of the long sea
an English music box
framed in modern metal
painted in the Mexican manner
by a Frenchman
spins Scarlatti in the air.

Oceanic valley
fetid aesthetical afternoon.

waiting at gate–Honolulu airport
elderly lady
short white hair
neck and noggin moving
to piped faux
reggae groove
or moving
in a Parkinson's tremor
later, same lady
grooving to faux
reggae
diluting cover
"come go with me"
so not
Parkinson's
a music
lover

Six Poems After the Honolulu Peace Conference

1

leave
people
room

2

The Meditation Master

the meditation master
chanting   shantih   shantih
peace   peace
glowered
at the upstart
kids
goofing in the front row
get quiet or clear
out! he said
the rest of you
breathe with half a nose
awhile
and focus
on this little flame I brought

3

we can shed our violent
selves don't you
think so
he said, don't you
think so, hey
I'm talking to you

4

protest blood
poured on military
records
smoldering
reactor fuel

5

8 day anti-nuclear
peace conference
with four days
half life

6

witness
for peace
but who
has seen it

Alzheimer's

(March, 1998)

I first got Alzheimer's
late one Tuesday afternoon
as the Honolulu sun slanted
the lanai and the leaves
and bracts of bougainvillea
stirred by sudden Kona winds
flickered in silver and shadow
and the shrieks of mynah birds
and gutturals of mourning doves
startled from the monkeypod trees
pierced the dusky air
at 5:17 pm February 23, 1992.
Later, because of the Alzheimer's
I forgot I got Alzheimer's
so I'm ok now

A Haole Writes One Local Poem

My granmoddah wen fish
catch one trout
trout?
haole fish, dat
she trow back

catch one snappa den
hapa fish
bitta
she trow back

granmoddah den
catch one ***
a local fish
pure you know
good fo eat
good fo da soul
granny keep em

*** (Look up name of good local fish)

The Condo Marxist

The drainage of the fens
of England is deplorable
she tells me
don't you think so?
she's here in Honolulu
for lectures and a book
on land and water
and to clean her real
fee simple condominium
by herself
to make it labor
intensive
deplorable, I tell her
you would have liked
all the former duck
swamps we are standing on

The Ride to Ho'omaluhia

as the tide rises and the rain-
waters ride the red cliffs
to fill the low land
and the bay of Kane'ohe swells
to take back the town, the roads
and the builders there
you can find peace
and safety, shade, stillness
the awe and power of sacred
protection
at Ho'omaluhia
you can ride out the tide
of steel and fossil fuel
and can ride the wave of conservancy
and botanic respect
you can ride the new maps
of the artists of Ho'omaluhia
tracing delicate cartographies
among the human the plant
and the otherwise natural world
you can take these rides yourself
at Ho'omaluhia and everywhere
and as always
bring your own horse

On the Ambulance Run

On the ambulance run the red scream
always startles
liquescent light a pulse
throbbing the hotel walls
the cool surface of the Ala Wai

On the ambulance run six or eight
prowl cars crowd a driveway
an apartment lights up, the ambulance
ebbs away
and for hours figures on the seventh floor
move from room to room

On the ambulance run the night
never blackens and the brackish air
stings the mind alert
Later on television the woman
whose husband startled a burglar
says yes I'd return
there's murder in Alberta too

‖ Jazz Note ‖

> "The point must be clear by now: that
> it is repetition, modified in one way
> or another, that gives poetry its
> musical qualities, because repetition
> is so essential to music itself."
>
> Leonard Bernstein

The trades up, those long cool winds across
the Pacific, as Ramsey Lewis's set starts
here in the Waikiki Shell. Repetition compulsions.
A retarded adult girl in front of me, moves
the seat next to her back and forth, back and
forth, my own repetition compulsions, form in writing
and form in music, even improvisatory free jazz,
requires resolution of sets, of anticipations,
Mailer's story of the man touching the doorknob
again before leaving the house in the morning
to feel the energy later through the metal
on the subway, repetitive
touch compulsion, the spirit in the steel, animism
in the modern world, and then the adult girl
the woman moves again, moves the seat next to her
back and forth and looks around a bit, maybe
she's not so retarded, not severely, her
movements certainly not fine, not exact
not apparently appropriate, the seat moving
back and forth, looking about in particular
blankness in her face, low affect the docs
call it, a blankness denser than the average
blankness on the average face on any dull
and blank and average day. Day after impenetrable
day, here just off Waikiki as the trades flare
cool Pacific evening back, hearing
Ramsey Lewis playing pure jazz again

When You're at Koke'e

"A party of five volunteers took to the field Dec.
20 for the West Kaua'i–Koke'e Christmas Bird
count. They recorded 1134 birds representing
33 species," as reported in the Koke'e Natural
History Museum Report.

When you're at Koke'e
number yourself among the fortunate
who ride the wave
of conservancy and avian respect
on Kaua'i
where people count
because the rare
birds matter

The Light on Monhegan, on Kauai

for Reuben Tam

let's say you are at your ease
of a late morning, an early afternoon
you've spent
the morning on Monhegan, on Kauai
and the afternoon light
moves in
over mountain, over blood cell
the slow afternoon sea

how
could it all look
how could you record it
or know
what the light is, or

where you are, precisely
amidst the pull of stars
and the salt and the tides
between the ridge stone in gold light
and the late day algae sparkle

the vast rolling spinning accumulation
of our ignorance
of where
the day is in its light
what the day is
and what picture
or word
could tell it

on Diamond Head, the morning rain
has started
swept leeward by the daily trades
which certainly will later sweep
across this rock
some blue and white amazing sky

On Mauna Kea

On Mauna Kea   fire mountain
    burst in fury from the sea
the sky, as everywhere, is Greek

    below the frost line
feral sheep scour the lava rock
    for pili grass

    further
on the high slope
    folkloric astronomers
record the semiotic night
    through a light dust of tropical snow

Meanwhile I Just Said to Myself

"Meanwhile," I just said to myself,
"as I'm trying to write something about
how the Dominican sisters slapped
me around and everyone else I
went to grammar school with, and how
it used to mean nothing, but how
lately novels I've read
and movies I've seen
Eddie Coyle by Higgins, Breslin
Pacino in Scarecrow, even Dedalus in Portrait
slapped and knuckle-busted, victimized
by nuns and Jesuits
lately, have made newly
urgent, meaningful and
symbolic all that Dominican
slapdash discipline I merely took
for granted
meanwhile
the cool semi-tropical dawn
has just broken over Diamond Head
a block and a half from my apartment
and a clatter of birds I could never name
just burst from a dozen trees
I know only as the coconut palms and
the assorted shorter ones
(Diamond Head is corny
unless you find yourself living there
five thousand miles from Brooklyn
an ecological ignoramus)
and the rain has started
swept leeward by the daily trades
which certainly will later sweep some
blue and white amazing sky

across this rock
and while the window runs
with rain and I watch the blurring
of the brooding cone beyond it
and in the next room, Laura
is still sleeping
I remind myself
that history, volcanic or my own
leads up to now, today
and though that article on nuns and novels
may have something in it
I think
right now
I'll write this poem instead."

II. Synaptic Trails

The night tide
rises
the moon
swells with light

A Biological Theory of History

It's this:
a cellular malevolence
insinuating through the spirit
like an inky pollution of the gene pool,
marshalling corruption
bringing men to their knees
producing murders and perky cocksuckers,
an almost inexplicable event
pollution of spirit and men on their knees
a cellular insinuation.

Could you flog a woman's pregnant belly?
slash an infant's throat?
the aesthetics of horror is just another subject
for an essay by Susan Sontag
in a century in which Artaud
couldn't cross the English Channel
without a strait-jacket,
and Eichmann turned to ex post facto Kant
to answer for dismembered sweethearts.
There are still deaths no one's dreamed of dying,
genetic pollutions and Channel crossings and
inexplicable sucking of cock to come;
who can pay the debt French letters owes de Sade?
the keepers of the pool, perhaps, who tried
the murderous chlorine of Calvin and Luther,
or Torquemada's up-front choice:
short-term death, or long-term dying.

What primeval terror has the gentle man known–
      what unambiguous vision?   contrivance of his own
What secure summation consoles the gentle man
      or cathartic demon purge
      anesthetizes source of sights
      or brings his eyes to rest?
         takes much to still a darting eye
         cauterize a plague.

An orderly attunement, fantasy to sense, with things bright
      things harmonious and savored with half smile . . . .
all sacrificial gifts, the gentle man knows
Though he's but a paying guest   contrivance of his home.

Bashing Neanderthals

it's anthropologically incorrect
to bash neanderthals
a perfectly fine species
never bothered anyone
never mocked a mammoth
for being too wooly
never looked down
their highbrow noses
at those less prehensile
and therefore could not evolve
for neanderthals such kindliness
was a rule of thumb
sure, they never slid a mouse around
to enter the world
of Bill Gates
who can get twelve million poems
onto the head of a chip
but who never spent an hour
with one any poem
not one hour
with any poem
so even in the cyber-cretinization
of e-language
bashing neanderthals
is incorrect

Nerve Stone Discourse

(for Rosetta)

cairns, cromlechs, steles
signposts
in the ancient meadows
link synaptic trails
over your cortex
like a roadmap of the Red Sea

with but crude lines to follow
the pre-frontal archeologist
sets sounding plumbs
to roust the past:
"Set it up again, Jack"
"All five million years?"
"What else, pal.
I aint up here for my health!"

down through neolithic
paleolithic all kinds lithic
of or pertaining to stone
through volumes of neural lace
dense enough
to hold your history

sweet concretions
in the mind
more earnest than a lunatic's request
these lithic talks adduce
the blithe calculus
of your unthinkable self

Biopoetics

In Hawaii we are well past
regionalism, that vestigial
aloha chat
to the new poetic
controversy, whether blood or nerve
is wiser
and through all the trendy blather
about left-brain/right-brain
a side issue
I've long thought the truly useful discourse
in American poetry would be
back-brain/fore-brain
why the hypothalamic fear
of cortex?

Construction in Congratulations to the Electronic Bi-ped Striding Toward the Frontiers of Language

1. "The visual (the perceptual mode of the man raised on print) makes for the explicit, the uniform, and the sequential in painting, in poetry, in logic, in history. The non-literate modes are implicit, simultaneous, and discontinuous, whether in the primitive past or the electronic present."

2.Athetosis: damage to local ganglia as opposed to pure spasticity, damage to pyramidal system.

3. GOOOOOOR! GOOOOOOOOOO! GOOOOOOOOOR! GRAHHH! GRAHH! GRAHH! Grah Gooooor! Ghahh! Graarr! Greeeeer!

    Grayowhr!

    Greeeeee

4. Double Athetosis: He could not stand, sit or hold up his head; could not move by rolling from one place to another; could not manipulate or grasp an object unaided. Could not speak, but indicated by direction of gaze, by smiles, and crude nods of the head that he recognized objects and pictures, later words.

5. Tendency to stiffen the body, and to throw the head backward due to spasm of the cervical and spinal muscles.

6. Vocalization: one month—ah, eh, na.
                     two months—gutterals as ga,
                         groo, roo, but not the
                         consonants b-p. d-t.

7. Rabbi Mendel's hasidim once sat at his table in silence. The
   silence was so profound that one could hear the fly on the
   wall. After grace the rabbi of Biala said to his neighbor:
   "What a table we had today! I was probed so deeply that I
   thought my veins would burst, but I managed to hold out
   and answer every question I was asked."

                     McLuhan, McClure, Tales
                     of Hasidim and a textbook
                     on neurological disorders.

Experimental Language

An Investigation of Eye Movement
During the Autokinetic Phenomenon
Utilizing Electrically Recorded Changes
in the Corneal–Retinal Potential
                    Exploratory Behavior
                in Cockroaches
                        (Blatta Orientalis)
            The Ability of Human Subjects
            to Attend to Visual Stimuli
            Not Centrally Fixated
        Sign Stimuli Affecting Aggressive Behavior
        in the Cichlid Fish
            (Cichlasoma Meeki)
                            The Nature of Love
                            Love-objects and
                                Surrogates

Adding "Poetry" to Chaos Theory
to Find a Poem

Suppose you have concocted a mathematical
model in biology or economics "poetry"
you put this model on your computer
and you discover
a Feigenbaum period-doubling cascade
which is often a sign
that chaos is present
is this result interesting?

well, probably not
one reason is that the detailed
dynamical properties of your model
may not have anything to do
with the properties of the real-life system

another reason why your discovery may be
without interest
is that the occurrence
of a Feigenbaum cascade
need not have any particular
biological or economic "poetry" significance
you still have to address the problem
of the relevance of your finding
for biology or economics "poetry"

David Ruelle, Professor of Theoretical
Physics   PHYSICS TODAY, July 1994

Oldenburg, Heisenberg and Oscar "Shotgun" Albarado

What counts in what we
know about a thing
is how
we got to know it,
what the instruments
of measure
were.

Sluggish distance, geographically
is miles
while weightless computations
charting stars, require
we call distance
years.

Time of day is told by
burning rope, or falling sand
shadows on a stone
or wheels fitted close
and set in motion.

Today in Pasadena
Oldenburg's exhibit
showed me this again,
that form alone
describes an object,
knowing objects
by a name, or use
is indeterminate.
"The Trowel is a hard version
of the swans
that live in the lagoons...

and relates also
to the Good Humor Bar
the Door Handle
and is an exotic form
of the Ray Gun."
"The Geometric Mouse
contains a human face."

"banana=fan
typewriter eraser=tornado
ice cream cone=punching bag
fire plug=ionic column
ice bag=fried egg"

Tonight I stopped off
in a bar on Pico
where the tv screen
showed rated welter
Shotgun Albarado
pounding out an
easy win
over some kid up from Hermosillo.
"The fights," the barkeep told me
"you can always tell
it's Thursday."

Man Alone the Beast

47 million termites
             swarm
      my 60 watt bulb in Kapahulu

I try to love nature
          and nature
     poets tell me wolves
         say, kill
necessarily, predators
           are non-intentional

          scorpions
have no Hiroshima
        rats
no Dresdens
         vultures, Belsens
         barracudas, crucifixions
nature poets tell me
        man alone
has killer mind

I try to love
        the food chain
animal murder
        as transfer of protein

nature
        poets tell me
calling cops pigs
        insults pigs
whales
        are tuneful
crickets wise

gulls
                screech overviews
        monkeys sign direct
                and uncorrupted

nature
                poets say subhuman
        assassination god's
                plan
        man alone the beast

        so as I spray and spray
        my 60 watt bulb
        typewriter, desk
        and window on Kapahulu tonight
        I feel
        quite natural.

Hawk and Rock

I hate hawks. Dumb
bird brain
symbols of elemental
wisdom. Falcons also
starlings, eagles
all alike
sappy creatures
spinning wings

and rocks, mute
omniscient stone
stacked, as rough coast
against some storming
hokey ocean
I hate also.

Give me the city
and the fierce bright self-regarding
poems of Jeffers.

On Idealization of Nature

if one were to photograph
nature
all nature, all kingdoms
of animal and plant
in stills, in video and film
and were to assemble all stills
and video and film
into one master movie
called <u>NATURE</u>
it would be the greatest
snuff film
ever made

What To Do With Scenery
                        (after Merwin)

Plan to see it
make particular arrangements to see it
travel to it
and see it
savor seeing it
savor having seen it
reflect   there was a time it was unseen
by anyone
reflect   there was a time it was unseen
by you
consider how you were
before you saw it
consider how you were
seeing it
consider how you
are
for having seen it
transform it
from the unseen to the seen
transform yourself
from never having seen it
to seeing it
to having seen it
and having seen it
picture it
there's more to do with scenery
than meets the eye

what else to do with scenery

having never heard of it
and on your way somewhere else
come upon it accidentally
truly see it

scraps of black plastic
amid perfect rows
of pineapple

III. *Only If Something Matters*

in my brother's coat
walking on a winter lake
old rain below

Some Guy Named Ludwig

When Frederick Jameson, third
or fourth generation Marxist
(is Jameson still trendy?)
proclaimed there no longer
are "writers or artists as solitary geniuses"
Richard Rorty replied "Freddy,
speak for your self"
Who wrote Beethoven's symphonies?
The collective cultural ethos of his times
or some guy named Ludwig?
What is the personal exclusive self
of Johann Sebastian Bach —
chopped liver?
Was it the downtrodden and threadbare
socio-economic deprivation
of underdog South L.A.
that created the Mingus Dynasty
or one particular singular gent
named Charles?

Turning Over in His Grave

The guy who wrote the original Tibetan
Book of the Dead
must be spinning like a lathe
tucked in the Himalayas
wizened scrawny and profound
in life, Do Not This, Thee
Rather, Thou, Do That
(transcribed)
since he heard the word
that D-lysergic alka seltzer
cures the planetary youth
of government and money
parents, other bringdowns
scratchy LP's
fascist deans
unamplified guitars
the world of strife and woe
the stateside planetary revolution in
the Sixties doing 42 choruses
of "Nobody Knows the Trouble I've Seen."
Like a gyroscope, I tell you
deep in those mountains.

The Phoenix Myth

would be less romantic
if we learned the bird
smokes in bed
and lives
in the next apartment

Celestial Mechanics

I'm an intimate of all fall down,
this drug regarding solitude
warms me like a sudden sun
not altogether healthy
for the silent scream that's in it,
every pore a vacuum as
my flesh is swept by solar winds.

The curse of one's most private mood
turns elliptical and clean
and turns again, bursting speeding and renewed
generating poem, or dance,
or quiet rioting
with staring at the wall.

I read this poem about geometry
or shadows
or was it poetics, or
some analogy among the three–
that sounds right
a poem about science and art
itself some artful connection
opting for the poem of course (being a poem) slyly
saying math's impure
or at least not pure enough
for one geometer not impressed by Euclid
or more impressed by non-Euclid
or some such twist
and what gets me, why I mention this at all, is
that the poem was good

though no one bled directly in it
words were clean, scientific
stitched in artful lines for the anthologist
and while a slashed wrist would have to wait
this poem of shadows, or math
or some connection in the courtyard of art
this fragile suture, poet to geometer, takes life
over your dead body
and mine

and it was good
which is why I mention this at all.

Dr. Patterson Speaks with Koko Before an Audience of International Scientists

thank you all for coming today
see how Koko's eyes are roaming the crowd?
that means she's glad to see you
she's connecting with you
see how her left arm and right arm
are outstretched?
she's saying the entire world
is connected and one
see how her fingers are curled?
that means Kant was essentially right
now she pumps her right arm slowly
she's saying Aquinas understood
the nature of god but
as she pumps her arm more quickly
she's saying Aquinas thought such matters
are ultimately unknowable by
the finite human mind
now by putting one hand over the other
she's saying that regarding the passage of time
Heraclitus was more correct
than Empedocles
now as she puts her left hand
to her mouth she's saying
she wants a banana
by grimacing now she's saying
your questions are difficult to understand
since human language is imprecise
now by putting her left toes in her mouth
she's saying to the anthropologist from Spain
that Cervantes is a great writer
and *vaya con dios, amigo*

now see her nodding her head to the side?
she's saying she's tired and wants to sleep
see how she's scratching her right buttock
as she saunters away? she's saying
that regarding everything she's told you today
she doesn't give a rat's ass
if you believe her or not

Sad Tropes

"There's a sadness at the heart of things
but it's hard to say sad in a poem"

Sad as a man writing a three volume
response to Freud
entitled *What Women Want*
while his wife
in the next room...

Sad as a man writing a three volume
response to Freud
entitled *What Women Want*
while his wife
in the next town...

Sad as a Marxist personally cleaning
her investment condo
to make it labor intensive

Sad as a lifetime subscription to *TV Guide*

Sad as the minutes of a meeting of a fan club

Sad as a historian who's got the facts wrong

Sad as game pieces by Parker Brothers

Sad as the perpetrator of a hoax

Sad as the logo on the stationery of an adoption agency

Sad as a man pricing pet food

Sad as a defrocked nun who's still a virgin

Sad as a rock fan playing a record backwards
to hear Satan's message

Sad as visiting hours

Sad as a royalty check for *Das Kapital*

Sad as brain scans of Grace Kelly

Sad as a hoedown in a hospice

Sad as a humanist asking his girlfriend to whip him

Sad as a prisoner whose case is declined by Amnesty International

Sad as a feminist settling in with a sugar daddy

Sad as a sugar daddy

Sad as a man selling maps to the G spot

Sad as an unwritten rule in the creative writing club
that all poems must mention the creative writing teacher

Sad as a class reunion in a sexual dysfunction clinic where
dozens were invited and nobody came

Sad as a writer whose only article
is entitled "Why I Write"

Sad as a writer whose only book
is entitled *The Writer's Life*

Sad as being arrested for resisting arrest

Sad as a tinhorn translator whose own poetry
shows a pallid metalloid ear

Sad as a man who walks into a psychiatrist's office
and says, "doctor, nobody ever pays any attention to me"
and the doctor says, "next"

Sad as a projected sequel to sad tropes

Say Jazz

to the jazz documentary film-
maker
who announces he no longer
uses the word jazz
go ahead use the word jazz
it's ok the word jazz
afro-american music might mean
jazz
docu-verite might mean
movie
use the word
you want
the jazz men the music
makers
who say don't say jazz
don't own the word jazz
they don't own the word
jazz
use the word jazz
if you want to
don't lose
your words
don't shuffle
your words away
use the words you want
say jazz if you want to
say jazz if
you want to say jazz
say jazz

Not the Uppers or the Downers

Though these are dangerous
enough, what kills
for most is not
the uppers or the downers
but the sideways
the days
and days
of sideways

Papa's Existential Etiquette

Do the spiritually correct thing
      be tough gracefully
      conquer fish
      victimize the maladroit
      defeat wine list and cheeses
      skewer beef in the afternoon sun
      acknowledge no master
                            but the shotgun.
                            the chill of waste.
                            the dread of jissom dried
                            up inside.

You are
      what you do
      the sum of your past
      how you make love
                            a scrotum of poses
                            burst in Idaho.

You are, finally
      how it all looks.

To the Author of "To My Brother Miguel"

Cesar Vallejo
           broken, like slow prey
                in the aftermath of tigers
passing the sunlit portion of dead afternoons
           on the family bench, bricked
                in victim recollections

can no sooner strike that shadow
           he noticed on his soul
than can Miguel re-enter August
                or John, November
             sunlight, night
or mustering memoriams reconvene
           childhood postures
           to fill the empty places
                in the playground.

I know this. And how some dead
           turn to fodder
              for the poems,
and that Miguel's elusive
           past all art, Cesar
and how the sunlight on an empty place
           is subsequent,
and not much help.

But your persistence.
           Muted lifetime over-
              turning stones
           in parlors, entrance halls and corridors
striking down the mountains
           to Lima and Paris
                and familial Spain

solitary, stricken with sparrows
        dealing well
        not so much with dead Miguel
            but with the subsequence.

This, I would come to know.
        And so
I join your hide-and-seek
        and keep to the shadows
            myself.

The Edward Hopper Retrospective

The man's dead
so I suppose that any looking
at the paintings
must be backwards
though I read someplace that
even when alive, he often held
the paintings back
unsigned, few dates
stuck in back rooms
didn't say much about it
never spoke much at all
married late, precipitating
his sensual period
painted the wife a few times
and let her do the talking
when the guests dropped by.

Today in Pasadena, two earnest gents
with full gray heads
one electric as Einstein's
both in shirts and slacks pressed
sharp and clean as the neighborhood Chinese
could squeeze it
scuttle and murmur through this gallery.
Old Left, I figure
readers of Fearing
totalling between them maybe
six or eight votes for Norman Thomas.
"He said it right in this one,"
one gent says
and the other nods
and they both stand there
looking and nodding

at a barren gas station
on the wall in Pasadena ——
and I'm thinking
what do these gray gents see
that famous Hopper loneliness
some moody Americana?
do they picture Tom Joad stopping for a fill-up?
Dillinger knocking over the joint for pocket money?
what did Hopper trigger right in that one
something from a film or book?
or some gas station they remember
thirty, forty years ago.

That solitary painter, these eminent gents
an art museum in Pasadena.
I try to find
the proper retrospective.

Early Onset

(after Antler)

early onset arthritic ice pick stabs
early onset short term memory loss
early onset long term memory loss
early onset belly fat hanging over
belt buckle
early onset hairline shin stress fractures
trying to run off belly fat
early onset permanent poet enemies
for running off
at the mouth
though saying true things
"on poets on poets"
early onset mild liver dysfunction
early onset no pattern at all baldness
early onset Catholic existential guilt
for two guys
in N'awlins and four
guys of Brooklyn youth
who will never be seen
early onset puzzlement at nurse practitioner
who recommends I check myself
for testicular cancer
early onset utter squareness
for replacing earlier
dextro-amphetamine sulfate
coke line or opium pipe
with Centrum Silver multi-vitamins
ah, early onset bleak solace
that early
onset means
I'm still youthful

Heraclitus once

Heraclitus once
was here
and said
things change

near the end
of his life he changed
his mind and said
nothing

ever really changes
then he was no
longer here

Between a Rock and Mahatma Gandhi

Between a rock and Mahatma Gandhi
which is better?

a rock is a perfectly fine
aggregation
of sub-atomic particles
Mahatma Gandhi alive is a perfectly
fine aggregation
of sub-atomic particles

a rock has rock sentience
Gandhi has Gandhi sentience

it's not better to be a rock
or to be Gandhi
if nothing matters

we have powerful personal knowledge
that nothing matters
suicide knows nothing matters
war knows and torture
the tools of the torturer know
extinct species know nothing matters
opium knows
metallic concentrates in the brain
stunned by Alzheimer's know
your house on fire while you are at the movies
the deepest inner thoughts of your great
grandfather's great great grandfather know
the room he was born in knows
the biochemistry of a cancer cell knows
the questions asked by Torquemada know
ashes scattered at sea

the digestive tract of the insect
feeding on the conqueror worm knows
the library at Alexandria
self-destructive habits know
an empty tube of spermicidal jelly knows
the temperature of the air in a Siberian prison cell knows
a neutron in an oxygen atom in
the ozone layer knows
the volume of Niagara Falls knows
the last centimeter of the distance between
this page and Alpha Centauri knows
nothing matters across all time and space
nothingness
knows nothing matters
nothingness knows most
nothing matters

though a case can be made
made every day
that something matters
though the proofs don't overwhelm

if something matters
only if something matters
Mahatma Gandhi is better than a rock

IV. *Poetry of Politics : Politics of Poetry*

witness
for peace
but who
has seen it

The Will Behind the Knife

If there's magic or miracle in sweetly
shot
seed driven with architectural grace
congealing in a moment pools
of history
sudden as a struck match,
then the will behind the knife
(a perfunctory collusion, you and me)
extracts its life from the silent dying
of that fleshly bit
scraped, liquescent and steaming
from its uterine repose,
quick and clean as the shelling of a clam.

A pale birth, without measure or miracle,
a ripple on the racial tide
clearly and doomed.

Semiotic Self-Deconstruction

Most theorists
of language
don't write very well
and their theories
don't tell them why

To the Manifesto Crowd

The insoluble quiz, the hard nugget
of doubt centered in every long, quiet walk
       taken to think things out,
              the proper dealing with adversity,
the reckoning with such as these: peripatetic
catfish, an angle on black humor, echo
chambers, vanishing tribes, seasonal time:
windy solstices blinking on and off
       like a metronome,
a dying sun hanging in bare tree limbs
like the pictograph for red,
ripe pear juice on your tongue versus
the neurophysiology of orgasm,
heroes (laws unto themselves) following laws
like pirates in home port
      ("avast, ye motherfucker! I'm the angel
of revolution!")
poetry sodden with prose,
advice to the old: "die"...to the young:
"kill,"
politicoes pressing the flesh
            "nail the edicts to the gate!"
you would interdict the finding of a voice
by techniques of inquisitorial persuasion.

The Socialist

He kept talking of Marx and hard times
how he was low on food
split pea soup and day old bread against
the winter
no rent
the battery on the old Volks cold
and the wife
plus Jesus now the kid

but I didn't buy it, this sad mix
of meager booty and rough breaks
for he also owned, he told me
one
seventy-five dollar dog
that's what he said he paid
$75
for a dog

now I understand seventy-five dollars
at top use
does not reduce
much misery and social grief

it makes no dent in famine
pestilence or plaque
a thin 75
bucks no tide of human villainy
I know historical
imperatives
take more cash

but for a dog
a Russian wolfhound!

(Lenin must be spinning like a lathe)
so as he sat there explaining
his personal brand of Mao
and scratching the ears of the mascot
of the revolution
I knew within his mongrel dialectics
there purred a fat cat heart.

Four Political Questions

Have you heard the rife effluvium
of the inadvertent junkie
a marshal
reduced by sudden habit
to primitive syntax of mock Indian
fork-tongued streetcorner Cochise:
"you fix me save you from pen?"

or Ronald Reagan?

Do you know that wily masochistic fish
who spurn the bait but love the hook
reduce their captors to
unsportsmen?

or the Electorate Way?

The Redistribution

Power
to the people
until they get it
then watch your ass
again.

The Suffix As Meaning

On the formation of meaning
in the language
of the Social Sciences

It's Germanic
that is, if you keep
adding a suffix
the word
eventually will make
new and powerful sense

A yalee anthropologist cites a tv ad as the principal
image of the Reagan years: a man in a white coat saying
"I'm not a doctor, but I play one on tv." Multiple
duplicities and deceits. (A yalee anthropologist?) A man
posing. Playing a pose. A poseur.

POSIT   to place or put, state a principle, or view

POSITION   as a noun, a thing placed, put, or stated
                 as a verb, to take a place, a locus of stating

                 as we get more sophisticated, we understand acts of

POSITIONING   as

POSITIONAL   stances, and more sophisticated still, we are wary
                 of

POSITIONALITY of a discourse or rhetoric, and must be vigilant
                 regarding

POSITIONALITIZATION of any utterance or set of utterances

> we just about run out of suffixes at this point
> reversing it, we can pare the thing down
> to its primary phoneme

PO   as a morpheme PO is an elemental chemical, a river
in Italy, and in Hawaiian, PO is the word for night
the ancient Hawaiian creation myth, the KUMULIPO,
tells of night as the source of the world, all origin
is located in the night. whereas,

POSITIONALITIZATION

> also is benighted, deep
> in the Social *soi disant* Sciences,
> nugatory, null, of meaning devoid

> [Tony,
> > Chinese meanings of PO:
> > > wave
> > > uncle
> > > cypress
> > > wide, vast...

> > > > yours,
> > > > Bonnie Mcdougall
> > > > (translator of Bei Dao)]

A YALEE ANTHROPOLOGIST
IN THE GERMANIC LINGUISTIC MODE

So you see,
             the statistics on marriage and divorce in Japan
             on marriages
             on marriageism
             on marriageizing
             on marriageality
             on marriagealitization

clearly show that divorce
             that divorces
             that divorceism
             that divorceizing
             that divorceality
             that divorcealitization

are socio-anthropologically related
             married one might say
             not divorced one might say

as anyone can plainly see
             from my data
             my datum
             my datism
             my datality
             my datalitization....

Hall of Fame

they keep Charlie Hustle
Pete Rose out
so far
for betting on sports
a multi-billion dollar handle
each American year
and for not telling the tax boys
all he knows
the other American pastime

while they hallow
good ole country boy
Enos Slaughter
you can guess what names
he grew up with
if Elvis
was the pelvis
good ole white boy rounding
first would try
to slash the heel
of Jackie Robinson
sharpened his spikes and tried
a quick swipe across the Achilles
tendon, tried to hurt him
end that boy's career
Enos Slaughter
Hall of Fame, 1985

Right Attack

Well just what IS the right attack
            for a poem
and what just doesn't go?
I've read the syntax boys
impersonal and cool:
            "A Voyage to Rangoon, after Forster"
            "My Favorite Analogue from Math"
they tell me madness now is out;
and the San Francisco finger circle
groping down Black Mountain
verses lubricated for each other's taste;
there's also something driven with the breath
tied up with meter
but like Doc Holliday
wheezing to an inconclusive end;
there's confessional
            but don't seek absolution,
beat, but make clear you've outgrown it,
acid-Tarot-vibratory-Tao
            sweet illiteracy
            cuz woids ain't so electrical as pic-chas;
and there's always the directions
like the South or West or numbers
such as Sixties, Nineties, forty-seven
other cults and bundles, modes
and apron strings, plus
of course the genius lone outsider
starving and unknown in Kansas
            or known and drunk on De Longpre.

A year ago I was having a beer in Brooklyn, around
noon in a neighborhood I didn't know. I was between
positions, cooling it and avoiding talk, when this
truckdriver, looking sold as a pump, slammed up to

the bar and ordered a boilermaker for his lunch. He was Italian, 2nd generation, of a tough and murderous half-crazed sort I'd known as a Brooklyn kid myself. A brutal nuts-stomping streetfighter, but too dumb to cut it as even a minor Mafioso, he might have done some small-change strongarm gigs for awhile before winding up on the docks, or hauling futile truckloads around New York all day. If ordered to he'd break both your legs, tho would always tip his hat to a nun. "The docs told me no more hard stuff, but fuck 'em," he said to me after his fourth, "the worst's already happened. Aint that right Angie, you was wit me." Angie gave a sullen nod over his beer. I figured he'd been with him, plus heard the story often. "Me and Angie was coming back from Jersey once last year, deliverin' pipe in East Orange. We got this empty rig, and I'm looking to make some time when all of a sudden there's this holy fucking pain in my guts like a hot knife. It doubles me over the wheel, but what could I do? I'm doin' sixty an' the traffic's pilin' up on the turnpike. Where am I gonna stop? Angie goes to grab the wheel but I say fuck it, I'll bring it in, I'm startin' to feel better a little. That's when I noticed what was happening, and I gotta admit, it fucking scared me. I begin to feel wet around the ass, and I look down and here's this blood on the seat and now it's dripping down to my feet. What the fuck could I do? There's no place to stop, so I figure to keep on driving to Brooklyn so's I could get to a doctor. Angie was getting scared too, you gotta admit that right? but I keep drivin'." Angie, long used to pointless intimidation, swallowed some more beer.

"And here's the part that's a bitch. It's something that I know now. I'm sittin' in this here pool of blood, feeling sticky. I start feeling weak too, and I keep on

getting weaker and weaker and feeling dreamy-like and
warm over the wheel. And you know what? I start feeling
n-ice! That's right, nice! Real weak and nice and relaxed.
Like nothing could bother me. I figured I was gonna
die but I didn't care. You know what? If you gotta die,
bleeding to death is it, pal. Bleeding to death is fucking
nice. "

OK. I don't know the right attack
any more than you
but I see that in the mags
the anthologies and schools,
the smug under-
ground tear sheets,
the mimeos and slicks,
wherever words are tacked up vertically
words
mostly bred from words
there's almost nothing
of that part that's a bitch.

The Teeth of the Mask

When I talked with Jack Lahui on his way back
to Port Moresby, Papua New Guinea
from his his third world or eighth world
literary invitation to poetry in Iowa
his first visit to America
he told me most everything was strange

he asked me at the Pali lookout here
on Oahu
"how many different
kinds of cars does America have?"
and why on stage in Iowa
a famous American poet
wears primitive masks?

I stood there in the Pali wind
American, and local guide
despairing of cross-cultural understanding–
I had just recently learned
that I'm a haole
and I didn't know how many kinds of cars
or about the poet in the mask
or why these were Jack's questions
or what my answers could have meant–
we drove on over to Kailua
in my 1965 six cylinder
light blue four door
Dodge Dart sedan

One

Apartheid rides South Africa
a mad unsteady Phaeton
hurtling toward desiccation
the long desert

This Man's Castle

The leader of
a group of Marines playing touch
football in the Bellows sand
says let's move down
so we don't interfere
with this man's castle

in a few weeks they'll be in Saudi Arabia
and maybe a few months later they'll
be dead, defending their homeland
their hearth, their inviolable
orders moving down the shifting
geo-politics of the New World Order
their blood draining
into the Saudi sand

Winslow Homer, War Illustrator

> "Historians suggest that after his
> blocks were printed the images
> were planed down, the blocks reused."

he had the stark angular death
cut deep into the wood
block, his drawings the surface

there, the quick pictures
of the illustrator, the journalist
images meant later to deepen

and stay, resonate
forewarn
before they were planed away

Sinēad O'Connor

svelte sensuous woman
liquid voice
of Innis Fodhla, ancient
Oirland, island
of destiny
fated
in the body
of Oirish masochistic
feminist political
warfare
to wear
as an emblem her
chemotherapy hairstyle

"Twenty cents and curtains"

("Nobody grows up in Brooklyn without learning
something about Sicily," Norman Mailer)

He thinks being mean is calling a
man a bad poet in
print or a fraud
a bland shit or
whatever, some verbal cut
but I grew up where
being mean to a man meant making a phone call to
a guy who made a phone call
to a guy
and the man was not seen
"Twenty cents and curtains."
The two phone call blast they called it.

Ivy Manoa

once in a while a yalee into wordsworth
discovers marx
and it's a revelation

for the yalee on oahu
had long wondered
why he has credit and his caddy

at Manoa Country Club
does not, you're my brother
he tells jeeves or bro in the clubhouse

if you need a nomination
to this place, bro
let me know, it's high time

it's well that we are well past
feudalism, bro, or jeeves, did you know
that poets know this too, bro

did you know
that wordsworth the voice
of the common

could not only talk like you
he could listen too?
what?

wordsworth
don't worry about it
a product like me and you

of the social economic historic
situation of his time
in his case an english guy then

in our case, bro, us now
wordsworth you and me, bro
brothers

Get Out of Poetry by Sundown

Just when I want to get tough
and excoriate something
false
say in politics the obvious false
of the Gingrich-Toffler contract
to dumb down America
or false
as the chemically enhanced
Hawai'i politico who swears
he just says no
or false as politicos anywhere with a straight face

or in music false
as a fusion cd by David Sanborn
or stone killer rappers
moving into the house of sit-coms
or false
as the numbing numbing drone of Philip Glass

or in movies false
as the bloodloving Salvador
a Rambo for liberals
or the Carver and Altman
sappy soaps of Short Cuts

or in poetry false
as silly Bunny Collins
perfect poet
laureate in the age
of Shrub

or in art false
as showbiz art
the geek chic of Laurie Anderson
the expressive neokindergarteners of Germany
the post-it stick-on

plates of Julian Schnabel
the anthrojive of Joe Kosuth
or earth
art with bulldozer palette

just when I feel I'm
getting tough like
cranky American soreheads
Rexroth on poets
or Mencken on the "Booboisie"

just when I'm feeling tough on culture
and politics and art
and am summoning new
language to say it new

I ask myself
what is this, a poem
or list of pet peeves?
what are you, the pot
calling the kettle black?
don't you know it takes one
to know one?
don't you understand people
who live in glass houses shouldn't throw stones?
haven't you heard to judge
not lest ye be judged?
in other words just who
the hell do you think you are?
if this loose talky poem is the best
you can do
get out of poetry by sundown

ok. I got tough again
I just wish
I'd leave me alone

The Survivalist

wild chickens
killed his parakeet
so he got his blade
dressed up
in a chicken suit
smeared himself
in parakeet shit
hid out in the underbrush
and waited
one tough
chicken suit parakeet shit
killer waiting
to split some chicken skulls with steel
waiting and
hiding out

On the Way to the Writing Workshop

the fiction teacher, creative division
saw cool writerly stuff
bees in his bonnet
still buzzing after thirty years
but did not let
the real
cat out of the bag
on the creatively writing
workshop scam
a toothless flea-bitten
lice-ridden pussy
that long ago
should have been put to sleep

On Bly on Poetry

In *The Sixties*, the mag
and the decade
Robert Bly
used to say there's no place
for wit
or humor in poetry
those British qualities
archaic and moribund
must
be kept
out
of the possibility
of a NEW AMERICAN
POETRY, American
poets I know
are still laughing about that

The New Formal Poetry

all the form
held
was the ruin
of the poem

Recollections of a Coot

I recollect Old Whitey
Bupkis, the hoariest
new voice in America
prospecting for a golden slowdown
in paradise
plumb deracinated he was
Bronx Angeleno cowboy
took to writing, damn good too
but then you know the fear
that starts to build around a man
he took to writing paeans to personnel
managers, "I sure admire the way
you handle death" he told a feller
and he died right there
just dropped, cold and hollow
though he was later seen
back in cowboy country
drifting over the low hills like smoke
when all the time all
he wanted
was room and board
in paradise

Poets in the Schools

Get the poets out of the schools
out
of the old age homes
prisons and kindergartens
get the writery residents
and visiting literateurs
off the cozy podiums
of the poesy circuit
"speak French and gerontology"
"interested in workshops"
"some Latin and Aztec and penal reform"
sweep these soi-disant
poets, these chattering bipeds off
the chummy groves
and get them back
behind the typer or the pen
and keep them there
until they come up with
some proof

Renshi (Linked Free Verse)
In The '90's

For Ooka Makoto and W.T.L., J.S., J.T.

I'll xerox the fax
can you fax the xerox?
I can hand deliver the xerox
if you xerox the fax
I'll hand deliver
the xerox of the fax
if you can xerox
the fax first
I'll xerox the hand delivery
then you fax it
I don't have a fax
then xerox it
and hand deliver it
I don't have hand delivery

too many hands ruin the poem
"too many hands ruin the poem?"

that's a good line
can I have a copy?
sure
I'll xerox it
and fax it to you
I want a copy too
in your own hand
I'll xerox it
fax it
hand deliver it
when that's done
I'll call you

I don't have a phone
no phone
no fax
no xerox
no hand delivery
to get in touch
truly
with one another
let's try
poetry

Snail Mail Poems

Date: Mon, 14 July 1997 dot Bastille 23:17:41-1000(HST)
From: Tony www dot Quagliano slash
        "creatively writing" dullards
        slash ethnicity mewlers
        slash blithery gibbery lit-crits
        slash any all frauds
        who give me pilikia
        dot aloha
To: Susan Schultz<sschultz@hawaii.edu>
Subject: Snail Mail Poems
        to
        the antipodes
        from
        the other antipodes
        will they ever
        get there?

pilikia–trouble

Short-Short on the New Anthology

"The promotion that is great
within us"

Poets, some
in it praise it
to the stars

others left
out say
it misses

major significances
in American
Poetry, it coulda

been more
and to be less
self

serving he shoulda
left out
himself

The New Lit Mag

Stop the presses! Stop the presses!
R. publishes T.!
T. publishes R.!
R. and T. publish B.!
B. reviews R. and T.!
Stop the presses!
Please

No Ideas But In Things

> "WCW is too surfacey. He's
> not deep like us."

No ideas but in things
or, as in the particular case
of the junior faculty english department
creative writing workshop guy
interviewing
the oldtimer english department
creative writing workshop guy–
no ideas at all

The Underground Press

"Poet" sounded pleasing
and so he typed fifteen
of his best efforts every year
and sent them to *Atlantic
Monthly, Harper's* and
New Yorker
and when the 45th rejection came
he fired off a scathing
outlaw note in verse
annihilating the *New Yorker*
and got instant publication
in the underground press.

Poetry Money

When I run into poet
friends published
for decades
in the littles
bigs, mediums and
mostly
the littles
here in Honolulu
or N'awlins, New York
or L.A., the most
frequently asked question
I get, is
"Any spare change, man?
I'm trying to make bus fare"
the rest
teach creative writing

The Travelling Regionalist

> "Get the essay on the jet
> before you talk about life"

Back when Hawaii time was slower
the proverb talking travelling
regionalist
might have set Hawaii writing back
a turn or two—
he'd been asked
to sing his father for a poetry
mag, but he said it's all there
in the mag, he'd rather
talk of region and province and the importance
of place
of fish and Alabama and how Texas
might be heaven
how a law degree is basic for an outlaw
how people moving into valleys
is bad for valleys
how Hawaii has a renaissance
how there's wisdom in the culture of canoes
how a certain catch in harmony
is like Flamenco or the blues
and how he's come to see this spirit of the region
everywhere-

back when Hawaii time was slower
we'd waste our time
on talk like this
not now
this aloha chat
substitute for father songs

this apologetic almost essay litters
our landscape, we want poems
on what the poet knows
what did he know
about his father?

Victory at Sea

the fiction writing workshop
teacher, creative division
saw the old war
on tv
likes tennis and diving
off Kailua, understands
the risk
of being human
is possible badness
and is now up to part three
of his trilogy
on the holocaust

You Can Tell "Creative Writers"

you can tell "creative writers"
are really writers
because they sometimes write books
called *Living the Writer's Life*
otherwise
it's hard to tell

The Showdown

The stranger stepped down from the stagecoach
and stood for a moment in the dusty street;
and few townspeople glanced at him quizzically
then moseyed on about their business,
deciding he was no threat.
He didn't appear to be packing any iron.
Then, in the fading twilight
the stranger strode over to the Last Chance Saloon.

"Which way to Stockholm?"
he said to the man polishing glasses behind the bar.

"Don't rightly recall no Stockholm in these parts,
stranger. Maybe you mean San Antone?"

Just then a voice
filled with cruel mirth
bellowed from across the room:
"HEY BOYS, THE DUDE'S LOST!
HAW HAW HAW."
It was Bad Bart, with six or eight of his gang.
"WHERE'S THAT YOU'RE HEADING, DUDE?
ALL FANCIED UP LIKE THAT.
HAW HAW HAW."

The stranger looked over at Bart.
"You talking to me?"

"HEY BOYS, THE DUDE WANTS TO KNOW IF I'M TALKING TO HIM.
HAW HAW HAW
MAYBE I'LL DO MY TALKING WITH THIS,"
and he slipped a glinting Bowie knife from his
boot and hurled it across the room.
It stuck in the floor between the stranger's feet.

The stranger ignored the Bowie
and stepped further down the bar.
"No, not San Antone. Stockholm.
Reckon I'll get directions later
from someone that knows."

"I know this territory pretty good, mister
and most of the people in it.
They call me Moxie."

"Glad to meet you," the stranger said,
not offering his own moniker.
"I'll have a bottle of sarsaparilla
and a glass."

"Sarsaparilla? Don't get much call for that,
but I recollect we do have some on hand."

"Much obliged."

"HEY BOYS, DID YOU HEAR THAT?
THE DUDE WANTS SASSPARILLY
LET'S SHOW HIM SOME <u>REAL</u> SASSPARILLY,'
and he filled a tumbler with straight whiskey
and walked up to the bar.
"NOW, I'M THE SOCIABLE TYPE, DUDE
AND I WANT YOU TO HAVE A DRINK WITH ME.
HERE, DRINK THIS."

"No thanks, friend. I've got my own."

"BOYS, I RECKON THE DUDE JUST DON'T COTTON TO REDEYE,
WELL, TRY SOME ANYWAY,"
and he splashed the full tumbler in the stranger's face.

"You shouldn't have done that."

"AW, DID I MESS UP YOUR CLOTHES?
THAT'S A SHAME. ALL THEM FANCY DUDS.
THEM SURE ARE RIGHT FANCY SHOES, TOO
AIN'T THEY, BOYS?
I WONDER IF THEY'S DANCING SHOES,
C'MON DUDE. LET'S SEE YOU DANCE."
and he whipped out his twin Colts
and peppered the floor around the stranger's feet
with smoking lead.

The stranger didn't move.

"Okay, friend," he said finally. "You've had your fun,"
and with cobra quickness
his hand darted to his inside jacket pocket
and emerged holding two sheets of paper.

"WHAT'S THIS?"

"Read it and weep," the stranger said,
"it's my acceptance speech for the
Nobel Prize in Literature.
I'm on my way to Sweden now
to pick it up."

"THE NOBEL PRIZE IN LITERATURE?"

A murmur broke out in the bar
and the rest of Bart's gang backed out the door.
"Your boys are hightailing it, Bart.
It's time for you to do the same."

"Jeez! The Nobel!"

The stranger's eyes narrowed to slits.
"That's right. For a lifetime
of poems and philosophy."

"Pomes?"

"You heard me, friend. Now make
your move or make tracks."

Bart's face glistened with sweat
and his voice was a whisper
as he turned to Moxie the barkeep:
"A six-pack of sassparilly, " he stammered,
"to go."

V. Word-Dance: For Poets and Poseurs

jazz rides
the cool trades here
in the Shell this evening
like spirit through steel
penetrating
the declining day

For Doctor WCW

Williams' courtly *Greeny Asphodel*
shows love triumphant
and poetry

triumphant, over the bomb
the blade, bullet, even the sting
of the quotidian bee.

Williams, the actual physician
in the actual thousand rooms
witness to the actual expirations

of his Jersey neighbors
knew disease as the actual depletion
and particular pain of the flesh.

Williams——who knew poetry cures
no actual illness
in the external world,

said if he were to write
in a larger way than
of the birds and flowers,

rather to write of those close
about him in all
the actual rooms——

would return from his rounds
in the declining days
to Flossie

his wife upon whom
so much
depended.

hardly a poem, a simple statement of the day's events:
cold dogs in the courtyard arrived in the morning mail
back cover photo of pocked and plagued Bukowski
hardmouth poet by admission
sap for crazy parlay: poetry and balls.
later, I stood around before a German class–
a fellow student told me that this Rilke guy we're reading
really led a screwed-up life,
sure, I said, he was alone a lot (I've already cast my lot with madmen,
should I defend them too from engineers?)
der Lehrer is a sweet Amazonian Madchen
taller than almost every man, her head, I'm sure, is ringing
with yelpings from the courtyard.
and now on the radio: sniping in Detroit
and Poitier reads Plato,
I do not invent this, there are hounds at every heel,
hierarchies of angels had no answers at Duino
Bukowski got drunk for ten years
and I sit behind a sorry six-pack
and sweat out hardly a poem.

An Occasional Poem To Czeslaw Milosz

Rereading *To Robinson Jeffers*, on hearing at 6:10 a.m., Oahu
time, Milosz got the Nobel
over Mailer and Graham Greene, you say Jeffers
did not know what you know
and that Jeffers' sky
was galaxies of violence and destruction
while Slavic
poets are children longing
for the Kingdom at hand
and that it's better to carve planets in wood
in the soft districts, to carve
more futile creeds
than to proclaim some dead inhuman thing

but only in the pure ferocities of Jeffers
does your poem take life
fired by the cold stars
your poem near dead from scholarship
and the fear
in bookish strategies

I think Jeffers knew what earth teaches
as well as the nakedness of elements
that a poem stuck in the world's thought
is a human thing
as for Hekate, Erinyes, Wotan, and Thor
zealous Lithuanian, Agamemnon
and the white kolkhoz tablecloth
I'll have to look them up

**13 Ways Of Avoiding
A Derivative Poetry Cliché**

1 – don't even start

On Asked for Writing Advice

write
with precision, lucidity and exactitude
in the sure knowledge
you will live to see
everyone you've ever loved
lovers, brothers, deepest friends
lovers
die
or
you will die first
which also
is very annoying

Ezra Pound in Hawaii

Fascist Pound unmournable
poet
Pound now doomed
to canto boosters
internationalistic cryptoethnics
fans of cultural collision
thickening usurious confusion

On Detractors of Kerouac

david wasting his sobriety
castigating wine and jack
whose anywork is magnum
and four quantum
leaps superior
to everywork
by ever dimming ray

Letter From Hawaii To David Ray

"Some dead
turn to fodder
for the poems"

Dear Dave
    first thought best thought
Kerouac said   here's what
I want to tell you

forget that grief group you let slip
you are in
no one there will tell you

you will be permanently sad and stricken and at times
unaccountably tearful and perplexed and ravaged
beyond the slightest sweet remorse at what
could you have done better

more things will happen in between
but you will never get over it
not poems or let's face it wonderful wine or the sour
calvinist avoidance

or music or orgasm or chemical derived from poppy
or coca or cannabis or collection of new writing
though most of these are quite fine and well sought

but after these and during and certainly in between
you will be stricken
with pure wordless sadness because Sam is dead

good popular words like heartbroke or arcane solace
like buddhist definition that birth is pain
death is pain
life is birth and death

or oklahoma christianity or particle physics models
of energy exchange or whatever anyone finds useful
will be useful
enough in their run

wanted to tell you
as we rode around Hawaii those weeks
past the pineapple fields on the high plain of leilehua
past the tropic lightning barracks
of James Jones you knew back east
or at the thin waterfall on the hana road
we paused for you to drink from
as the dark folded in
everyone solicitous
your son dead
the entire counterclockwise spin in Hawaii
your sorrow palpable
$$\text{your friend}$$
$$\text{Tony}$$

On Bukowski Elegies
and the Dipshit Clowns
Who Write Them

Mike B. Edsel: "*New York
Quarterly* might
go for this, I was at
this lawn party, see
Buk was there
Buke rhymes with puke
Buk rhymes with fuck
Buke rhymes with puke
Buk rhymes with fuck
and me looking nifty
in my radical
American Flag sneakers"

On Andrei Codrescu's "Writers"

"A writer friend of mine told me..."

The story almost certainly not
Malamud more
likely Frank Harris
if so, Andrei, stop
hanging with the ignorant
I said the same to
Bukowski once and he understood
exactly

The Night I Let Bukowski Live
(for Neeli Cherry)

I

Jackie Leonard
used to tell of the time
he was a lifeguard
"You were a lifeguard?"
"Sure, at Coney Island"
"Did you ever save anybody's life?"
"Sure, I remember one time
a man was flailing his arms
and yelling help! help!
his noggin bobbing there
in the waves
no one else saw him or heard him
the ocean was rough
I rushed in, cut through
the powerful riptide
and when I got close
I threw a hatchet at his head
and missed
it saved his life"

II

at the apartment of Linda King
that night of the party
of Love Poems
when I let two fools rush in
to save Buk's life
my car didn't start
but luckily, I had
my blue ox outside
saddled and tethered
to a Silverlake palm tree
and I rumbled home
in the cool L.A. dawn

another of the wisdom boys
flapped into town last week
a jovial buzzard
with a huge rep
picking other people's flesh
other people's bones

while here
he hung out with the health fooders
and at the Showtime
Pizza in Aina Haina
where he asked his host
what is that music
the robot animals are playing?
"it's called rock and roll, sir"
he was told

87 years of sentience and experience
still, I guess now I won't ask him
who put the bo
in the bo-bo-bo bo-bo
who put the ram
in the ram-a-lama-ding-dang?

Bunny Mullins Poet Laureate
Not in My Name

poetry for soccer moms and security moms
[Robert Penn Warren is spinning like a lathe]

Silly Bunny Mullins
is the perfect poet
laureate in the age of shrub
Bunny like Boy George
light
weight
ill-informed, good
smiler, glad hander, a people
person with the skills
to climb, to cultivate Academy of
American Poets, Poetry Society of
America, Association of Writing Programs,
ill educated,
likable, a lettuce eater,
flag waver
charming, enduring, cute
beacon for
poesy programs
and champ of "creative writing programs"
flatterer
Bunny Mullins
Bunny
Mullins
Laureate
not in my name

A Fable for "Creative Writers"

the boy poet from the south
goes to New York
to rendezvous
with big bad Broadway Dan
Broadway Dan
gets the boy poet from the south
very drunk
and takes him
to a seedy hotel
in Manhattan
where they spend the night
talking philosophy
and art and literature
and practicing safe poetry
next morning
the boy poet from the south
wakens and blinks and says
"Broadway Dan?"
"yes, boy poet from the south"
"Broadway Dan, why did you take me
to this seedy hotel in Manhattan?"
"well, boy poet
this is not any seedy hotel
Delmore Schwartz once stayed here"
"Delmore Schwartz stayed here?
he did? actually here? he did?"
"why, yes, boy poet
I knew you'd like that"
"Oh, Broadway Dan
you know me so well!"
beamed the boy poet
and he's been practicing
safe poetry
ever after

on new academics foisting a new moronicity

Myles says Billy Lame-o is Thoreau
because Lame-o likes
the outdoors
Lame-boy Billy
buffalo chippies
Walden Pond, and ooh
the outdoors

sour spam says Saijo
is Blake, not
just _like_ Blake, _is_
Blake, because Saijo
uses an actual pen
and Saijo actually
quotes Blake
ooh, this boy is Blake

such is just some
of the new moronics
the new moronicity
new creative writing
in America, generations
of new moronicity

Hard Guy in the Faculty Lounge
(on Philip Levine, who cares for people)

Ignorant at 19, he confesses
brief fan of Jeffers
sounds certainly true

but the longer
story is his ignorance
since

of music and depth
and the self
delusions of people

who proclaim they love people
"Jeffers didn't care
for the people I care for

oh! I care for
the common
the real"

tough working stiff labor
agitator thirty years
in the English Department

"I demand we teach Swados'
'On the Line'
or I walk!

I insist
else my tues/thurs
class is through

and I demand
a new sofa
for the faculty lounge"

Who's the Real Slim Talent

The real m & m blue boy
               [as James Brown, the godfather of soul]

who's the real slim talent
uh-huh, uh-huh
the new blue boy
uh-huh, uh huh
slim talent
slim talent
blue m & m
uh huh uh huh
slim talent
slim talent
the new blue boy
uh huh, uh huh
new ofay boy
slim boy
playing black

uh huh, uh huh

the real slim white boy
the new blue boy [age 30, age 30]
playing black

uh huh uh huh

blue boy playing black

uh huh uh huh

and who're the real
slim nitwits
uh huh uh huh

slim nitwits
slim nitwits
sucking it up

uh huh
uh huh uh huh

the real slim nitwits

uh huh

Some Boondockers

slickers
of hickness
hauling canned food
to the mountains

pondscum singers and
wrongway rubes
pining
for opera in the outback

haulers of sprouts and granola
through the mean streets of Marathon

prairie fires of confusion
the mealy stagnant thickening
confusion Ezra sed
would kill the singers
and the song

Language Poet at the Baseball Game

I arrived late and asked him
"What's the score"?
"Flub-a-dub and a scrum
two touchdowns and a par six over
a net without tennis
by a furlong and a nose
overtime and 3-point play
outside the paint
3-point play
what's the point?
if I could follow the puck
a nor'easter took the squall
to skiff
flubbity skiffity do
and someone made an error"
Yes, I thought,
your creative writing teacher

On Poetry
  (after Ogden Nash)

Duende is trendy
but leaner is keener

Andrei's Shtick on Letterman

or why he never looked at the monitor

goot eeevening, ladies and germs
what sweet music
Paul Shaffer makes
I am from Transylvania
in Romania
a small fang-shaped country
my English was bad, very bad
how bad was it?
it was so bad
that in Rome
I would say
"go kill yourself"
but seriously
Transylvania, yes
vampires
they are my tribe
that is why
I do not see myself
in the monitor
I do not like mirrors
you fools!
but seriously
fangs you very much
I just wanna tell ya.....

Raymond Chandler

now and then some new punk
with a pen in L.A.
tries to cut
Raymond Chandler
born in Chicago and at seven
taken to England for an education
where he learned
to get back to the States to make some green
in the black gold of Redondo
and El Segundo the L.A. frontier
learned there the dreary
factual dullness of American money
having it or not
quit in his mid-forties
to write stories the first
in Black Mask in 1933
23 short stories and seven novels
later, plus some screen work
and advice on writing:
"if you get stuck
have a man come through a door with a gun"
he had invoked, invented and set forth
Los Angeles

many writers have written well
superbly even surgically
on that peculiar ciudad
Nathanael West, Fitzgerald, Evelyn
Waugh, Joan Didion, Aldous
Huxley, Charles Bukowski
but it's Chandler's "hard pale wild lilac hills"
seen from the city
the dough of Brentwood and Beverly Hills
the rot of Bunker Hill and tinsel glittertown

end of the continent desperation
the beach towns
the quiet murderous dark
suburbs
electric red winds off the desert
placid housewives lingering
over the kitchen knife and contemplating
their husband's neck
the L.A. state of mind

and Marlowe the big combo of Paladin
and Henry Miller's criminal-artist
told in The Cosmological Eye
(Miller never read detective stories, hated them)
the loner investigator ethicist Paladin
damsels in distress dames in trouble
hated by cops as a solitary
while to punks, blackmailers, killers, thieves
to rapists, slashers, gunsels
to the greedy, mean, and let's say it
to the evil
Marlowe's just a cop
so his help comes when help comes at all
from the outside, the margin
"I can't say we'll stay healthy Marlowe
but here's something you should know..."
more guts and integrity in the low
than a mansionful of dough and power
Bogey the best Marlowe
of the five or six American masks

Marlowe
moving through
the hordes of crooked cops

appointed judges who play along
fast buck dealers in land and water
starlets and stars sold out or eager to sell
nouveau riche and old rich, anybody
on the make on the climb
Marlowe
moving through
the dull brutal bloodlit
city, where the sun could explode
like an icepick in your brain
sappy romantic
doing what he can
to get right the precise features
of the mean world
paying his price
moving through in the orange light

Investigative Reporter

It would take an invisible
reporter
like Joe McGinniss
to sidle up to Jeff
MacDonald in the yard some day
or library, real casual
and ask Jeff if he'd ever read
"The Dream Team"

In the TV GUIDE story on "Fatal Vision"
MacDonald selected Joe McGinniss
to write his life
because of Joe's old Philly story
on a triple killer

I'd guess instead
MacDonald knows Joe's "Dream Team"
a sad tale of good wine
bad luck and champion
ponies, blue grass
Florida sun
the chance in it all
bright flamingos in the dawn

and the albatross
the dull
wings beating
the woman
as murder
victim

no one dies
in Joe's dream
in Jeff's
the kids were next

The Genius Award for a Life's Work
Of Elaborated Signage

goes
to a Texas redneck
writing secondary
commentary
on art
on painting
on sculpture
on the history
and philosophy
of it all, while
himself not
creating any
not one
image at all

genius commentator
his own life's
work essentially
elaborated signage

it's cool
to be declared
a genius
but what
if the judges
were morons

Feed the Hungry, or
Do Something Better
(On H.L. Hix in H.R. Six)

give a man a fish
he's fed for a day
teach a man to fish
he's fed for life

aphoristic
even apodictic

while the actual
starving wander the actual
world out

of earshot
of neo-beatific
sermons

Last Chance Poem for Wing Tek Lum

"Poetry is rare in Hawaii
as everywhere"

Do you still want to be a poet?
get strong
hate haole, if necessary
hate Europe
Wing Tek, a real poet
writing like a sad ass grandma
half a dozen years
"my keiki showed me her coloring book
ooh, the rainbow!"
do you still want to be a poet?
get strong
three thousand years
of genius Chinese poetry
Wing Tek, kick
the arrested development of Bamboo Ridge
out of your skull
kick out
all the puerile whining
of small keed timers Eril and Darrek
get strong
kick out
all the ethnicity mewling
"oh, whitey done us wrong"
hate me, if necessary
ask, *demand*, who the hell am I
to tell you what to write
what to think
about writing
what is this?
new whitey paternal
attempt at cultural control?

hate me, if useful, Wing Tek
colonial Tony, luna on horseback
herding all the sad slaves
then, get strong
don't be a Bamboo Baby
forever, get strong
"be angry at the sun" for shining
be angry at the night
last chance, Wing Tek
be a poet
again

keiki–child
luna–plantation overseer

Kesey on Kerouac on TV

Ken Kesey strides
late in 1983, November exactly
onto the Letterman Show
like a tough Truman Capote
in a formal suit
and hemp hat
and rolling
a big hemp ball
getting all the giggly hemp
laughs of any Cheech and Chong
let's all stay eleven
forever routine
to plug his article on Kerouac
in Esquire

I started looking for the issue right away
Kerouac the worthy
subject, and Kesey
in print can be brilliant
and certainly above
hemp punk expropriation
and while there's Kerouac's and Cassady's scorn
of sixties hippie groupies
to consider
and Jack's researches
on vampires

still Kesey on the Letterman Show
is no more himself the writer
than Kerouac on Steve Allen
talked into talking of the long rolls
of printer's stock
he writes on

time's a little slower
in Hawaii, the new Esquire
is not in yet
I'm looking forward to it
I feel that Kesey on Kerouac
in writing
would get it right

To Kerouac

to Jack as the story goes
to Jack jazzloving Jack of the bebop prose and soulful poem
to Jack of the heart as huge as the beauty of jazz
to Jack the visions of Gerard
to Jack this novel a mix of dream and memory and idealization
to Jack the diamond light poignancy
to Jack love and grief for Gerard
to Jack forlorn meditations on mortality
to Jack illusoriness of all appearances
to Jack of the greater poignancy
to Jack intimations of his own unworthiness
to Jack wintry emptiness in his own nature
to Jack his "dead man heart"
to Jack writing Gerard visions at age 33
to Jack of the heart inhabiting "a cold indifferent lair"
to Jack "sick in my papers"
to Jack "the whole reason why I ever wrote at all"
to Jack "because of Gerard, the idealism, Gerard the religious hero"
to Jack everything dies
to Jack the transience of being
to Jack Ti Jean visions of bliss
to Jack peace beyond grief
to Jack the wintry heart where grief dies

Benjamin Latrobe in New Orleans

I

The Sociology of Apocalyptic Deliriums

      bat device registered in Latrobe's brain
the architect's hallucinated fiend
      had class
                        high temperature
sugar distillation
      Bacardi
                        high class norte del rio
      low class bat swill below
the fever along the nerve of the descending staircase
green wine in a beached shell

II

Apocalyptic Poetics

      old style:
            they say it was the yellow fever killed him
            or was it he was yellow all his life

      new:
            the long fear

Ezra's ABC's, and Deeds

"Ezra was nutty, but very kind"
JL, 3/92

Let the image strike the mind
            leaping   line
cobra to throat
reader apprehended
            fieldmouse
                        struck
by nighthawk   owl
            any raider
talk in tongues
      and know yr history
Sing

Days in private music
            spring
                        the word-dance
looking straight within the heart
                        tightest words
fitted equal
            to the scrolls of dynasties
            or tunes of troubadours
                        starburst signatures
      for lutanist
            or emperor
unwobbling pivot of the weal
      or just for kicking up the heels

Dichten-condensare, bastids!
images impacted as a fang
make yr woids a picture

shovel-shot like jimmy joyce or otherwise
direct, just soaz I get ya
oh, and re the gold flow...

Politics
    a burning prairie
war songs on Il Duce's mike
                    the key
    to Pisan cages and St. Liz
and in the cantos
    shredded history and broken glass
cultural collision
    private talking
fishbone sense

Illimitable Country

"Each artist's strictly illimitable country
is himself"

> E. E. C. in a public letter in
> defense of Ezra Pound

when the power boys
were changing Ezra's cage
from Pisa to St. Liz
and hordes of mute
poets watched
it was Cummings
cartographer of the heart
who mapped
and publicly proclaimed
his old friend
Ezra's
true terrain

One for WCW at the Post-Nuclear Philosophy Conference in Manoa

Greeny *Asphodel,* light triumphant
love triumphant and poetry
even old courtly devices, when useful,
triumphant

by bomb, blade, bullet or
hyperallergic bee sting
all the old bones will go
ah, but will they dance before?

Willy sawbones went out
cutting a rug
the actual doctor in the actual thousand rooms
witnessing the actual thousand expirations

of actual Jersey neighbors
their sub-atomic particles rearranged in
entropic configurations of disease
the fire draining out

to cool light
and imagination
and while poetry
can't do much about it

the thing is
          poetry
               does the most

VI. Poetry Overheard

one still treescape
a truck back-
fires
87 birds change trees

Wolfsbane for Cantwell

Everybody needs an ace
especially in what the shrinks
might call
a high stress situation
so in Basic Training
at the Infantry Training Center
Ft. Dix New Jersey
home of the ultimate weapon
Private James C. Cantwell's
solitary ace
was his clearly much practiced
and cherished
impression of Bela Lugosi

For weeks he spoke only like Lugosi
quoting that classic movie
adapting the phrases for every situation:
"Inspection, Cantwell. You'd better shave."
"I do not like mirrors. You fools!"
or someone would saunter into the dayroom
and from the far pool table:
"Gut eeevening, Mis-ter Harr-ker"
or in the barracks after lights out
everyone exhausted and quiet, settling in
there'd come that Transylvanian trill:
"Listen to the children of the night!
What sweet music...*they* make!"

It was after weeks of this that Manny Tranquilli
who stuck exclusively with the three guys
he joined up with from his neighborhood
in Newark, New Jersey
and who hinted at mobster connections, said:
"This jerkoff Cantwell's getting on my nerves"

"You'd better be careful, Manny," I told him
"they say a vampire has got the strength of ten"
"Sheet. That yo-yo ain't got the strength of *one*,
 some day I'm gonna do him up good, Newark-style."

Which of course was Tranquilli's ace
the old neighborhood
where he had some power
owned a .38
and would dip his wick when the time came
The movie roles *he* favored
were by Cagney, Garfield
E.G. Robinson and Duke Mantee.

But most of the platoon
let Cantwell play it out
often feeding straight lines
as in the mess hall:
"Hey, Cantwell. Want some coffee?"
"I do not drrrink....coffee."
or when Ramirez
from the bunk above Cantwell's
went on sick call looking pale and weak
Privates Muniz and Ortega swore
they saw two tiny punctures in his neck
and about a dozen guys
took to wearing crucifixes
on their dogtag chains

So Cantwell must have thought the guys
were clowning
that night when four of them
appeared around his bunk
"Gut eeevening, you fools!"

he greeted them
before one crushed a pillow
to his face
while the others pinned his limbs
and punched and pounded on his belly
and his chest with savagery, efficiency
and malice

Cantwell couldn't make the reveille formation
and when the medics rolled his stretcher out
with his suspected broken ribs and
severe internal injuries
he didn't say a word
to any one of us
in any voice at all

Intro to Camarillo Kate

"I was afraid of the cars the cars frightened me
Camarillo State just like a jail you're locked up
and getting out, at first everything is frightening
it's so easy to be in jail . . ."
(I'd been talking of Anne Sexton
                              in the loony bin
ah horrible, talk of sanity!
something we can take hold of)
sure, the bartender said
I'd guess it would do something to you
                              I suppose it would have its effect;
the dollface whore spoke of two years
                              in Nevada State Prison a boyfriend had done
it had its effect, she noted, in flesh lost
and then, suspended, Camarillo Kate turned to the face:
"Are you Dutch? Put my finger in the dike."
                              She licked her lips.

And bought a six-pack and left,
walking.

Real Class

She looked good in the cafe
out of place, you know
so I took her to my apartment
"Oh, that music is beautiful. What's it called?"
"Moonlight Sonata," I told her
"named after an Italian prostitute"
she laughed
we had a few drinks
and everything went fine

but in the morning she was gone
with all the lire in my wallet
and my entire collection
of Beethoven.

Post Op

a pin in the hip of the night nurse
who brings me weak codeine
her boyfriend she says
as big as me
stumbled and crushed her
here, she touches herself
her white slacks taut
on her hip tight on her thigh

I'm only just now getting back to work
she says, are you
better now? the mild narcosis

I'm routine here, a lower
right quadrant abdominal
an "appy" they say in the halls
sleep spreading and the night
nurse has blue mascara
and wants to talk

another nurse
brings ice for the face
of my roommate
his bleeding cancerous face
does the tv bother you, he asks me
I'm lost without it

the room clears and the night
nurse reappears, my boyfriend
she says, didn't mean it
and what counts is
I'm working again and

walking fine now, don't you think?
she moves across the room
in the tv light

here, she says, offering
a codeine-4 in a small white cup
I know how hard it is to sleep

Getting By

–for Harold Norse

No food for three
days, simple as that.
Soon
I'll haul my scoured ribs
past the final talons,
past Villon's wolf jaws
feasting on air,
past Vallejo's Paris days,
past Arab mouths
snapping the wind,
past what's good for you,
Appalachian tragedies,
eaglet faces torqued to the sky,
past saints who chose this route
this indignity, this simple third
or eighth or twenty-seventh day without food.
I could beg coins
or like Kafka's artist
charge admission,
I could minimize
bread alone,
I could stitch a life from this
or call it art. I
could haul my scoured ribs
past politics and find wine
in an empty belly's mockery
of government. I could side
with such romance
or really, I could tell you
that I live in Los Angeles
weigh two-thirty-five and just
shared a mushroom pizza

with a lady on Vermont Avenue.
We had five bottles of Bud
and now I'm going for some rum,
Bacardi light, with Coke and limes.
Cuba Libres. Sausages for breakfast.
Ah, my friend, did you really swallow
all that bitter deprivation?

Her Blues

(a true story
she told me)

"'how she's gonna explain this black baby
to her other three white kids?'
well damn
she shoulda thought of that before she
opened her damn legs, meanwhile I'm working
with three of my own plus supporting Joe
but
I was willing to raise it cause it was his
so the county people checked me and said my *own* place
was too small and took me to court to keep my *own*
is what I get for being nice.
more than one Caucasian dude is crazy about me
one been through college in architecture
and I've always been able to pass
and I've had it with Joe the bastard though I loved him once
I'm ready for something drastic, really.
she's long gone now of course
and Joe's still here and I'm tired, really.
my mother was white my father's mother was white
but chalk dudes always find out about my blackass kids.
if I knew at fourteen what I know now at 23,
really."

At the Artiste Bar
the barmaid's mouth sets
against laughter, she
talks through her hands
and her quick fingertips suture her smile–
she can't forget those missing teeth–

not even later, I wonder, her arms and legs
spidered over some guy's back
eyes wild or quiet in penetration
what shape has her mouth then?

Shack Job

Nobody lives
with a shack job
I don't know anyone
living now
with a shack job
a shack job is someone
you <u>used</u> to live with
never now
your friends acknowledge this also
nobody ever says
"How's your shack job?"
or, "I'm having a party Friday, man
why don't you make it
and bring your shack job"

        "Get lewd for a blow?" she asked? "No dice, boss."
        [perspicacity and the snow-blind kid]

it's always your old lady
or your woman or girlfriend
or lover or mistress or cohabitant
or sometimes your wife
and in this room right now
a beautiful young lady is sleeping
and I watch her and am grateful
that I'm not her shack job
either.

        [perspicacity and the snow-blind kid]

How I know
that obscure lady
ain't worth too much:
Lady
if I could just recall
your name
I'd dedicate
this poem
to you.

The Typo in the Tattoo Parlor
L-O-V-E and H-A-T-S

was my fault
I arrived too early
for my article with Sailor Dan
the tattoo man
on what fools still get
tattoos in this time
of poison blood
poison spikes
when the fad is over, Dan
the skin, the poison
remains

arrived early to talk
with Dan from San Diego
on his new pictorial ideas
ask how's our friend Harley
"Deep Ink" Davidson of Oakland
and how's southwest Louisiana
needle maestro
Boozoo Dopsie the Cajun
Picasso of skin

too early at Dan's new crib
off Hotel Street Honolulu
I startled him and
he slipped, lost it
working the knuckles
of a white boy
nouveau gangsta
Eminem, Vanilla Ice
if you get my drift

who wanted L-O-V-E
on the left knuckles
and H-A-T-E on the right
in deepest ink
that can never
be lasered away
but Sailor slipped
and wrote H-A-T-S

the gangsta, one tough
customer has made the best of it
knowing it's all about style
and a signature
so he shows righteous L-O-V-E
when he delivers knuckle sandwiches
and on the other hand
sports a glove

and also always sports
a cool array
of very way cool
hats

The Great Turtle Priest on Television

When I was twenty years ago
on pleasure in America
they did as they pleased and called it
Zen
that was their understanding
of Zen
they are ignorant
and benighted
such thinking is not true Zen
not at all
Ah! Doing calligraphy!
I'll pay my doctor's bill with this one
I'll sell this for
cauterization
and acupuncture
the others
the television crew can have.
The law of Buddha
and the law of business
is the same.
Great Turtle....
our hats hide us from the world.
The bringing of women into Zen
has been a question
like the eating of meat.
It would be like other sects
if they had used the word "Buddha"
it would smell too much of Buddhism.
Here, my private home in the mountains
a follower gave me
two hundred years old
I'll probably die here
though I haven't had time for a night.

Everything here in the mountains
takes twice as long as the city.
Zen and I
Tachibana Taiki
Chief Abbot
Temple Daitoku, Kyoto
Great Turtle Priest.

Medical News on the Night

medical news on the night
radio says treatment
of the retarded especially
those not severely
only mildly
is difficult
because they
know
they are retarded, know
it will be difficult
to find someone who will love them romantically
and knowing it
they become sad

those only mildly know
it will be difficult
the medical news at night
those not severely
it's difficult
though not severe
everywhere there's so much worse
(40,000 babies died today Oct. 4, 1990
abuse, starvation disease, pre-
natal, post-natal, natal, dead Oct. 5, 1990)
on the night radio the retarded
know, the mildly
it will be difficult
(Oct. 6)
the radio news they know
it will be difficult to find someone who will love them
romantically
and knowing it
they become sad

For Carl Furillo
(3/8/22 to 1/21/89)

In Ebbets nobody took third
on the Reading Rifle in right
he could throw a lamb chop past a wolf
as they say
right field in Ebbets had the 25° angle
that was Carl's wall
and behind it was Bedford the avenue
of Carlo's partner, Duke
Carlo was proud he went all the way up
to eighth grade
no college, no high school
batting champ in '53 at .344
an ironworker, and after Brooklyn
a guard for a grocery and deli
with good benefits, security
Carl you got leukemia he recalled
the doctor saying
I'm not saying he was the first
anybody ever said that lamb chop
past a wolf about
I'm saying
he could do it
he could cut down
anybody foolish
trying to stretch

Making Light
> On three works in The Paper

> "Tragedy is easier than comedy
> because in tragedy all you have to do
> is say the baby died"

a man walks into a psychiatrist's office
and says doctor
it's my uncle, he thinks he's a chicken
your uncle thinks he's a chicken?
all day long, he acts like a chicken
he walks around like a chicken
he makes noises like a chicken
he thinks he's a chicken
have him see me, I think I can cure him
cure him? we don't want you to cure him, doctor
we need the eggs
Kira is the story of the bird-girl of summer camp
written with high seriousness, but the author
needs her eggs

but I wanna tell you
the baby died
extinguished in a small hotel room in Waikiki
how small was it?
the room was so small
I had to go outside to change my mind
the room was so small
all the flies were walking
and also the room was cold
you say the room was cold?
the room was so cold, that one morning
I fell out of bed and broke my pajamas
you're talking cold
but seriously, the baby died
the culture in place obliterated

by the culture on tour
take genocide, please
for nobility and virtue which side
of genocide?

stars of soaps are blessed
with tumors
the operation is a risk
or a lasting vice
to give longevity
for a poet on Puget Sound
brain dissolving to a puddle
the inextinguishable galaxies
are running lights in a small harbor
he clutches his wife
in a high window of their home
and somewhere near
the teary fraudulence of last-poems-left-behind
and the terrible inutility of wit
Blessing's poem
swells with light

At the Fairgrounds Bar

(N'awlins, 2003)

When the Giants lost
yesterday, I was with Jimmy
at his place
with five yards on it
and we went up
early
24 points!
I started to chirp
Jimmy's parrot
started to chirp
me and Jimmy's parrot
we was chirping
then comes the loss
after 24 up!
it was like a bad day
in the swamp
it hangs on me
like a snake around my leg

The Botanists

I'd been drinking since evening
                and now it was Tuesday
and earlier there'd been some speed,
                amphetamine, dextro-sulfate type
which does this sphincter trick
                like a fist snatching your sex
                from the inside,
and on top of this, the pig
                wasn't even pretty.

Okay, these were my excuses. And at dawn
                she said to me
"your cock's no tiger-lily
                is it baby"
and she pulled the sheets to her shoulders
                so's to say she was through.
I held her head then, sweet
                roseate bitch, and told her
how cute she was, a scorched sheath
                pinked with friction: "your cunt's a corpse
on a waving stem,"

but really I was thinking
                "no tiger-lily," what a thing to say!
under other circumstances, sweetheart
                you and I could get along.

The Wacko and the Shrink

at the exit like a bat out of nowhere
he pulls alongside

hey, fuck you! you fuck!
you cut me off!

what?

fuck you! fuck you!

his face livid, contorted horribly
he's bouncing in the seat
spittle on his chin

signs of possible parietal tumor
or hematological subdural pressure
trigger rage response
I'm thinking what a cat or cort scan would show
look, friend...

fuck you! fucker! die!
I know where you live!

sir, I recognize your anger
I've seen the causes...

fuck you! you fucker! die!

ok, now I recall why you look familiar
your face looks like your mother's cunt
which, by the way, smells like drano
take it easy, I'm not knocking the drano
after ten thousand sewer rats fucked your mama's pussy
why shouldn't she try to freshen up?

were all your mama's ratfuck children
cuntface cocksuckers like you?
or are you the only stinking ratfuck cocksucker
from your mama's cunt?
medical science is imperfect
and we may never know the final truth
in these matters
take care getting back onto the freeway
these are dangerous and confused and violent times

Deconstructing a Disgusting
Dirty Filthy Poem

"Your poem is filthy and disgusting
and I'm pleased to accept it for NYQ" (WP)*

it's on anger
and madness, escalation
of violence

on how language
of science
is latinate and elegant

while language of cursing
is anglo saxon
and harsh

on social
disintegration and the loss
of communitas

and mainly on animals
like bats, rats
and cats

*the response to William Packard's acceptance of
"The Wacko and the Shrink"

The Vapors

"Nobody loves you like your mother
and she could be jiving too"

(Blues lyric)

She said she was born with her guts in knots
twisted
nerves drenched in poison
her childhood a panic
of confusion
and hallucination
She said her mother hated
her, thought she was worthless
and told her so
often

Later, she said her lover
hated her, thought she was worthless
treated her lowdown and mean

Then she said she's had it and anybody
crosses her
there'll be blood
on the floor

Now nobody knows her like her mother
or lover
and I hardly know her at all
but now that I've met her
three or four times
I'm beginning to get their drift

Noir Letter to The Swede

for M., 3:20 a.m.

I knew The Swede was in trouble
I read his letter again to see what it was
but it was nothing in particular
bad booze maybe, trouble with a dame, the usual
too many nights closing Pedro's Black Star
the rotgut sauce. Pete the Mex
never did break out the Chivas
then The Swede back in his room
waking up at 2 in the afternoon
wondering what time is it
what town is it
doing a favor on his mind
he'd done me a favor, and I was grateful
he drew a blank on some information
I needed, but still I was grateful
in my business
I knew most everything leads nowhere

But I couldn't shake the idea
The Swede was in trouble
I read the letter again, and there
it was, a short line about
"that's the trouble with Italians"
The Swede was savvy and knew better
when his mind was right
he knew the last guy who said
"that's the trouble with Italians"
was Jimmy Hoffa. Right before Jimmy
became 12 cans of Alpo

The Swede was on a long slow slide
forty years talking a book
on the Harlem Renaissance

but no pages, no hard covers
nothing new at all
besides, that renaissance was over
a long time ago
like The Swede
still there was trouble
imminent exit and obliteration
so I'll see what I can do

Musial and the Bums

it was the Brooklyn fans of bums
who knew his class
and named him

those wait 'til next year
fans playing out each autumn
and winter like Brando

in Waterfront
"you saw some money kid
it just wasn't your night"

"my night! my night!
I coulda taken Wilson apart
you don't understand

I coulda had class
I coulda been somebody
instead of a bum

which is what I am"
fans of bums without envy
who knew his skill and majesty

his grace, Musial
man of springtime
Stan The Man

Sure, That's It

for John Garfield

Sure, sure that's it
you had it all figured out
you knew if I went to the club that night
I'd see Rico's car in the lot
and know he didn't leave town
like he said
he'd be at the bar
with his new babe, Brenda
I'd go in there to talk to him
about Murphy
you knew the cops took my gun
over the Shelton thing downtown
sure, that's it, you figured
I'd barge in anyway
and Brenda would be a witness
you knew Rico was scared
a real sweet set-up
wasn't it, sister
Rico would plug me
and Brenda would tell it to the cops
unarmed, see
and Rico would take the fall
real cute
with me and Rico out of the way
it would be clear sailing
how else could you get your hands on the Four Aces
so you're the one who sent me that note
to get me there
who else knew I'd be in San Pedro that day
real cute
just like you set up Shelton
you knew he's always at the fights on Thursday

he'd leave his shiny Packard
on Spring Street like always
he always gave some street kid four bits
to look after it for him
so you gave the kid a sawbuck
so he wouldn't look too hard
sure, that's it
you had the time to plant my hotel key
in the back seat
you knew after the scuffle in the Olympic
the cops would get around to me in time
and take my gun
you hired that chump to act drunk
maybe he was drunk
and insult Shelton's babe
grab at her and call her something
Shelton would go nuts
and the cops would be all over the place
so when I got that note in Fermin Park
that Rico might be at the Four Aces
you knew I'd go
real cute
but you didn't figure everything, sister
you knew Murphy saved my life in France
and there wasn't anything I wouldn't do
to square things for him
you counted on that
I don't always see eye to eye
with cops but Murphy was a good cop
and the way he died was wrong
and you knew I had to fix it
sure, that's it
you take something good and sometimes
you try to keep it good

they were saying Murphy went bad
and that I was part of it
but they were wrong
and so were you, sister
it's you who makes everything twisted and dirty
you knew plenty
but there's one thing you couldn't know
Murphy's wife, Jeannie
gave me his Silver Star and his .38 special
she said to me do something
so when Rico went for his Luger at the Aces
I drilled him
he's not dead
he's spilling his guts to the DA
and Brenda's talking too
so she was a good witness after all
but not the way you had it figured
was it, sweetheart
I can see how Shelton fell so hard
Shelton had a lot of dough but he was no chump
a woman like you
sure, that's it
guys think a woman like you is worth anything
Shelton thought that, and Rico
maybe I think that too

VII.   Illimitable Country:
Other Places, Other Poems

Ah, to be East
of the Apple
where the Islands
are Long
and life
(as everywhere)
is short

Brighton-Manhattan Transit

No romantic Howl, instead
the invisible sound of friend and flesh
whispering into mist
mingling with the wind
which drove the sharp-edged snowdrifts gathering
around stone tables in Washington Square Park,
where old men played chess by day
and passed the vegetative nights
in choking yellow rooms
thinking up tomorrow's gambit.

Across Crane's bridge, aerial fiber
arching object of more myth
we rode the chattering subway
to the end of the line
where the manic grin of Steeplechase's
pagan gargoyle announced amusement
at the heart of Coney Island.
And all the while
your empiricist insistence:
"What we know we know solely
in the sanctity of our senses."
But I saw your eyes
make little fearful gulps of wonder
as though recalling a nightmare.

Carnival Parlay

In Brooklyn's Red Hook
Puerto Rican street
dancers parlay muscatel
Caribbean color, drums
bandanas, roaring
phonographs and ruby port
into desperate carnivals
to occupy the August heat.

A cold walk home

under a flat moon
a frost spiked with old winters,
linked further in my dead brother's coat
worn first against the South Bend snow,
and on his own returns to Brooklyn,
then his own spiked and stirring nights, taken back.

On the phone today Sweet told me she was beaten
"my friend was drunk, and well, it wasn't pleasant."
Tell me about it.
"Not at all, but I'll see you tonight."

Krait coiled in the bedsheet
conventional horror has it
that you can't move
reptile death a batted
eyelash away furtive
malignancy cool on your belly
these parts see more cottonmouths
or cobras certainly
not kraits
icy paralytic
lizard vision

krait business straight
from television
you lost eighty pounds in two months
we watched *Stalag 17* awhile

returned for your belongings
in the restless dark
amazed with news that Wednesday
nights Pat went to the Apollo
in Harlem for the amateur show
your records, books, food in cans
scuba lead belt, blue Hong Kong
suit, letters, shoes, scientific
notes, experiments and poems
in progress loaded in Pat's station
wagon in the morning light
turnpike back to Brooklyn.

that November,
I went to Washington
with our father and his brother, Pat
to gather your belongings
I spent the night on an impromptu cot
in your living room
talking in the dark
with Uncle Pat who never really knew
you or me or Dad his brother
but who surprised me with the news
that Wednesday night he went to the Apollo
Theater in Harlem to catch the amateur show.
In the next morning's sunlight
Pat helped us bundle up
your records and your books, scuba gear
two suits, letters, assorted writings
scientific notes, shoes, journals
experiments and poems in progress.

soon after, we learned that Uncle Pat
had been himself the host
of cancer,
about two years worth.

A Brooklyn Dodger Fan in 1988

A Brooklyn Dodger fan in 1988
must feel as secretly stupid, as hopeless-
ly sentimental, as stuck in soft nostalgia
as childhood driven
as privately disengaged and backward-
looking
as any sports fan anytime
or anyone who thinks about
remembering

Color Line

The Dodgers said the line dies
forever
at second
and later in the World
Series in Los Angeles
they all wore black
armbands
for Junior
Gilliam Brooklyn Rookie
of the Year
pivot man known
forever down the long years
as Jim

A cold rain obscures L.A. tonight.
I'm driving the Harbor Freeway where
thick ocean mists
barely slow us below sixty,
rain is more rare
and we're stopped up now
a mile of us in our
cars nosing the sleek road.
I've heard this coast
attracts
the self-destructive,
I stylize my caution
an extra car-length
turn up my radio
and move toward an exit in the alien rain.
I'm not from here either.

No handle on the night
can't calculate the mood.

Anger ("that dumb bitch")
beneath it all, the nearest girl I love
was in my morning mail,
hysterical note "must talk, I'm cracking,"
you have a history of hypochondria, my dear
but if you're really pregnant...

It's hard to know one's moral obligations
among L.A.'s bare tits and eucalyptus trees.

At Western and Washington, a bust:
white cyclists against the wall
broken storefront window
three then eight proliferating prowl cars

Later in a go-go club almost everyone is black,
one black and foxy dancer does some of the positions
'til a big dumb white girl stands
vacuous and beautiful and dull
barely dancing, sifting flesh and silicone,
nembutal myth of earth and Marilyn
a fire both to Robert Graves contemplating Egypt
and Richard Speck shopping for a knife.

There was another place with roaches on the bar,
a masochistic faggot thumbing in the street,
a lawn party, and a letter to a poet
incalculable night ending in this
and if you're really pregnant....

Ancient Gringo Savvy

Mexico's insistent as a broken pact
        and unexpectedly
for I had some plan
    a sense of beach
        some clarity of nearness
    in the stars
        and in the woman with me
    desert to be sure
        but ocean too
sleeping bags for the cool evenings
    a small fire with beef on sticks
        red wine
        ice for beer
    perhaps a day on rented horses
    riding the sand dunes south of Rosarito
mutual laughter
        the permanence of cactus
    fishing coves off Guaymas
        mutuality in flesh, nearness.

A modest, pared design, with no corrida
    no museum of Aztec artifacts
        Olympic games
            or existential bulls,
and while hunger stretched the wide eyes
    of the children
        playing in the dust
            among the scattering chickens
    and old men squatted
        skeletal
            beside their roadside stands
        hawking ice cream or a crucifix
    and certain of their daughters struck
        other bargains in the towns

still
I'm no revolutionary
        nor even much political
knowing, with ancient gringo savvy
        that reform of men by politics
is a short scenario
        played out in a sniperscope.

Bone and root assassinate
lovers are knives
and skies
trick cactus into green suicides.

Bus Ride Notes

Rushing beers in Modesto
so as not to miss the bus
a staff sgt. to my left
through California valley, dark, in from the Pacific
passive bus rider, refugee, returnee (vacilando)
through the night to plastic L.A.
"perhaps a letter" thinks three-up-one-down
hence reputable and not so crazed
rushed beers ignite surer than cafe waiting
mellowness sought down the line
from incongruous San Francisco through
backyard Oakland past San Jose
whose college produced good boxers once
to Modesto where vegetables and fruits define
perimeters of an old bar couple's understanding of the land
needing only "room and board," they say
oh, and "drinks" and "fun"
(afterthoughts from the lady)
so as to make "room and board"
not so vegetative as the land.
Behind me a child about three sings:
"Jingle Bells
Jingle Bells
Jingle Bells, the way
Jingle Bells
Jingle Bells
Jingle Bells, the way"
reminding me that children
not to say you and me
don't learn too much all at once.

Driving Through Donner Pass

We backed up for that
portly hitchhiker
no anti-freeze
and it was starting to snow

take a magic word like tundra
or timber wolves
Malamute
or North Slope, Yukon
the gold lust days
from books of course, Service
the cremation, the shooting
rinky-tink dance hall
women crazy-eyed at the end of the earth
a place to go
whooping it up at the Malamute
the killer frost, and six-gun
from radio too, as a kid, I
heard King growl at the friendly trapper
long before good Sgt. Preston
found the miner bushwhacked and
the claim jumped
"should have figured, a trapper with no furs?"
so I can understand, Friend Prosak
the pull
the frozen purifying getaway
to leave the lady
and the son, the Pasha
pack it in, head north
maybe a pipeline job
the ice
for the first time in twenty years
no books, just like Thoreau
the ice
watch the ice, Friend Prosak
the long midnights
and those mother timber wolves.

Society Island

the owner of the Dahlia
outside Papeete
told me how in horror after
her New Year's drive
for luck around the island
she threw away the eggs she
bought by mistake from a leper
colony
near Taravao

Gauguin

in the fever and stunning
solitude in that tiny
hut on Hiva Oa
his last picture
showed Breton Snow

Papeete Poem

There's no escaping it
and to survive
you've got to drive the sad
romanticism from your heart
the wonder at what joy, what
sweet vaginal pacific bliss
what pelvic tender mercies
Annah the Javanese might be—
Gauguin in a bar fight for her
had his ankle stomped
someone had been rude
and back from the hospital
he found Annah
had cleaned out his studio
and left. Later, he wrote
his friend in France "My broken
ankle causes me great pain; I have
open sores that the doctor hasn't succeeded
in healing, and in the tropics
it's no joke"
You can't go to Papeete
without thinking of Gauguin—
When Gauguin's daughter died he stopped
writing his wife
he had trouble with money
and the authorities
and syphilis
the rot and fever and stunning
stunning solitude in that tiny
hut on Hiva Oa
becalmed at last under the
vast and aching sky—
His last picture showed a Breton Village
Under Snow
and his boldest portrait
masterwork of sensual repose
showed Annah the Javanese
in a blue chair

A Jazz Note

(N'awlins)

jazz rides
the breeze off the river
through the Quarter this evening
like spirit through steel
penetrating
the declining day

No Bullets in the Sky Tonight
N'awlins 12/31/2000

Party in peace
brothers tonight
here in N'awlins tonight
we got to
got to
party in peace
tonight brothers
leave your weapons in the crib
no weapons tonight
leave the weapons in the crib
no bullets in the sky tonight
which might could fall
on somebody might
could fall
on anybody in the night
party everybody
party in peace
leave the weapons in the crib
party in peace tonight
in N'awlins brothers
in peace brothers
no bullets in the sky tonight

Night Sky Piano

Walking from the Quarter
on Poydras, empty
deep night
a young man hesitant
approaches, avoids
eye contact
stops
before us, whirls
a 3/4 pirouette
stops
stares at the sky
raises his hands
his fingers
moving musically
playing the black spaces
the stars
playing the night
sky piano

Edward Hopper's Lighthouse at Two Lights, 1927

> The world about us would be desolate
> except for the world within us.
>
> - Wallace Stevens

a white lighthouse in the hard flat
white light of Maine
projected above the white clapboard

outbuildings, the dwellings
of the lighthouse man
bright on the hard coast

one warmer yellow house also
with an empty dark central window
a bit of low watery foliage

one brown chimney smokeless in summer
and in all, open empty windows
open empty doors

no one is pictured there
not in any of the doors
or any of the windows

where at most they would be between
the internal and external worlds
no one there to see what ships

go by at Two Lights
and for anyone on shipboard
no one there to be seen

Quick Cities of Shadows

In New Zealand the cultured gent
said "hmm, quite neo-Byzantine
with West African
mudhut overtones"

at Bellows east of Honolulu
as the keikis dug the burrows
and walls and smooth
shovelsful and scraper-shaped
forms of keiki-size cities

the passersby said Barry's city
is Egyptian
and Mayan
like a temple
a medieval fortress
something futuristic
an art deco movie set
what is it, exactly?
how long did it take?
I've seen something like it on the Maryland shore
at Cannon Beach, Oregon
every year in San Diego

as the light waned and the tide
turned on itself
to reclaim the town
Keiko said all that will remain
will be the memory
cities flickering like shadows
in the minds of the walkers on the beach
reclaimed from the long forgetfulness

To See Shoah

to see Shoah
nine and one half hours
you have to come back a second day
you notice not everyone comes back
you have avoided all reviews
and commentary but recollect
the director has been called obsessed
the minutes accumulate
there are trains and the schedules of trains
there are trees now and trees then
there is soil and its particular composition
there are shoes, teeth and smoke
there is the capacity of trains
and the capacity of buildings
there is a boy thankful for a job
there is a barber thankful for a skill
there is a farmer recalling watching trains
there are mounds of details
and you think about them
you think of Shoah for months
if you were born in 1941 in Brooklyn
you reflect this took place
as the snows fell on Sheepshead Bay
on Brighton and Coney Island the snows
fell in your childhood
you try to write something
on it and you feel profoundly false

Tony Quagliano

1941–2007

About the Author

TONY QUAGLIANO (1941–2007) was a poet, essayist, jazz writer, literary critic, editor, and professor of American Studies at the University of Hawaii and the Japan-America Institute for Management Science. He published widely in numerous literary journals.

Tony was born and raised in Brooklyn, New York. He received his BA in psychology from the University of Chicago (1963), where he published his work in vision research, "An Investigation of the Autokinetic Phenomenon." Living in Los Angeles while teaching at the University of Southern California in the 1960s and 1970s, Tony would sometimes hang out with Charles Bukowski and, in 1973, he edited the then-definitive *Small Press Review* special Bukowski issue.

In 1974 Tony and his wife, artist Laura Ruby, moved from Los Angeles to Honolulu. He completed his PhD (ABD) in American Studies at the University of Hawaii (1978) and there reconnected with Reuel Denney, a friend and mentor from their Chicago days. Tony created a tribute to Reuel in *Poetry Pilot* (Journal of The Academy of American Poets) Reuel Denney issue (1988) and edited the posthumous volume, *Feast of Strangers: Selected Prose and Poetry of Reuel Denney* (1999). He served as editor of *Kaimana–Literary Arts Hawai'i*, (Journal of the Hawaii Literary Arts Council) (1990-2007); and, was a contributing editor to *The Pushcart Prize: Best of the Small Presses* since its inaugural issue. Tony was a well known jazz writer and served as script consultant and poet for "Swingtime in Honolulu: The History of Jazz in Hawaii" for *Spectrum Hawaii* on KHET public television. He worked extensively with Laura Ruby, creating artist-writer collaborations and art exhibitions both in Hawaii and nationally. He was honored as one of six national jurors that selected the single haiku for the National Japanese American Memorial Foundation sculpture in Washington, D.C. (1997).

Hear Tony read his poetry:
hawaii.edu/lruby/artistwritercollab/artwritcolab.htm

Selected Awards and Honors

Academy of American Poets Prize (1967)

Clark Award in Poetry at University of Hawaii (1975)

Pushcart Prize–Best of the Small Presses Award (1976)

Honolulu City and County "Poetry on TheBUS" four-time winner (1985-1987)

John Unterecker Award in Poetry (1989)

Brussels Sprout Editor's Award (1992)

Azami Award (Osaka) (1993)

Mainichi Daily News Annual Award (Tokyo, Osaka, Kyoto) (1994)

Haiku Compass: Directions in the Poetical Map of U.S.A. (Tokyo: Haiku International Publishing). One of two poems selected to represent haiku in Hawaii for the 300th anniversary of Basho, in Tokyo (1994)

Elliott Cades Award for Literature (1999)

Stefan Baciu Award in Literature (2000)

Hawaii International Peace Day Poetry Award (2007)

About the Tony Quagliano Poetry Fund

The Tony Quagliano Poetry Fund honors Tony's lifetime commitment to literary excellence on the local, national, and international scenes. Tony's contributions to the world of poetry were many and wide-ranging. His was a singular voice in poetry: He reveled in the possibilities of language, the sounds of words, and the potential for philosophical complexities. Tony was feisty, humorous, joyfully exuberant, and had an inviolable sense of justice—and all of that in engaging poetry.

The fund acknowledges excellence in poetry through the Tony Quagliano International Poetry Award. The fund will further Tony's legacy through its support of NYQ Books™ and it will establish his literary archive at Temple University Libraries.

Tony Quagliano International Poetry Award

This award recognizes an accomplished poet with an outstanding body of cutting edge work.

To find out more about the Tony Quagliano Poetry Fund,
the Tony Quagliano International Poetry Award,
or to make a tax-deductible donation,
please visit our website:

tonyquaglianopoetryfund.com

Or write to:
The Tony Quagliano Poetry Fund
Hawai'i Community Foundation
827 Fort Street Mall
Honolulu, Hawai'i 96813-4317

www.hawaiicommunityfoundation.org

CPSIA information can be obtained at www.ICGtesting.com
Printed in the USA
BVOW072122290312

286433BV00001B/11/P